PRAISE F

Your Inner SHE-EO

"*Unleash Your Inner She-EO: Become the CEO of Your Life and Achieve Success and Fulfillment* isn't just another book, it's your personal guide to unlocking your true potential as a woman. Written by an author who is deeply passionate about empowering women, this heartfelt roadmap gives you the tools to overcome obstacles, break free from limitations, and achieve your full potential. You'll get more than just advice; you'll find a trusted companion who believes in your dreams and champions your journey toward success."

— Lisa Chapman, Screenwriter, *Heart of a Champion, Love on the Rise*

"Unleash Your Inner She-EO is a transformative book that empowers women to unlock their full potential and achieve success in all areas of life. Written with a focus on personal growth, professional development, and building a purposeful life, this guide provides practical strategies, insights, and inspiration to help women become the best versions of themselves."

— Karen LeBlanc, National TV Host of *The Design Tourist*, and anchor/producer of *Louisiana, the State We're In*

"As a woman in a male-dominated industry, I had to fight for everything I achieved. I understood the importance of seizing opportunities, accepting responsibility, and strongly believing in myself and my abilities. *Unleash Your Inner She-EO* speaks to these areas and serves as a guiding light for women seeking a successful and fulfilling life. This empowering read is a beacon of inspiration and practical applications that help guide women toward a future where success knows no bounds."

—Susan Dunnavant – COO – Concert Golf Partners and named one of the Top 10 Women Influencers in Golf

"Ivy's guidance for elevating to your full potential is a game changer. If you're wondering why success is evading you, or why your success isn't as satisfying as you expected, embrace this journey toward a more purposeful and happy life. After spending two decades laser-focused on my career, the concept of transforming from CEO to She-EO is energizing and inspiring. Take this step to widen your lens and bring more meaning to your life."

—Jennifer Breton, CEO Lebel & Harriman

"As someone who has experienced firsthand the extraordinary power of creating a compelling vision that entices you to take action and the power of a focused mindset to help you navigate life-altering circumstances while gritting it out day after day to reach your personal and professional goals, I found Ivy Gilbert's *Unleash Your Inner She-EO* relevant, compelling, and remarkably instructive. Her writing is painfully honest, and her desire to help others shines through."

— Scott Burrows, Speaker, and Author of *Vision Mindset Grit*

"A must-read book for all women who strive to excel in life. Ivy teaches the readers the inextricable link between doing inner, personal work and sustainable success. *Unleash Your Inner She-EO* leaves you feeling confident and empowered as a woman wanting to grow personally and professionally."

—Grace Van Berkum, Owner Gracious Living Lifestyle

"Ivy has a unique way of bringing important issues front and center. Her book made me realize I have been a She-EO since 1988. I held my own in the building contractor arena among my male counterparts. The reader will find encouragement, a road map, and a path any woman can follow to achieve what she once felt was unachievable. I was honored to co-author a book with best-seller, Ivy Gilbert. I learn something new each time I read one of her inspiring books."

—Brenda B. Keith, Published Author, Educator, Contractor

UNLEASH
Your Inner
SHE-EO

ALSO, BY IVY GILBERT

FICTION

Protectors of the Light

The Keeper of Clarity

The Power of Clarity

The Leon Redemption

Echoes of the Past

NON-FICTION / FICTION

Feeling Funkabulous: From Funky to Fabulous After Forty

NON-FICTION

Expiration Unknown: Planning for a Day No One
Wants to Plan For

Kindness Journal

Women's Financial Wisdom: How to Become a Woman of Wealth

IVY GILBERT

www.ivygilbert.com

UNLEASH
Your Inner
SHE-EO

Become the CEO of Your Life and

Achieve Success and Fulfillment

Ivy Gilbert

I dedicate this book as a tribute to my younger self, whose inner strength propelled me to pursue my aspirations and dreams. Moreover, I extend this dedication to my future self, confident that she will persistently embrace and fulfill her life's purpose.

TABLE OF CONTENTS

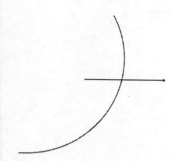

Foreword

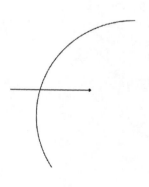

UNLEASH YOUR INNER SHE-EO

As you age, you tend to look back and ask yourself questions: Did I make the right choice at a particular juncture? Did I risk enough to achieve a goal? Did I go the extra mile to help an employee, a colleague, or a friend? Did I enjoy my work? Did I give back when I could? Am I proud of my life?

In order to have the right answers to these and other questions you ask yourself, you have to be in charge of your life. That's what *Unleash Your Inner She-EO* is all about. It provides you with step-by-step actions you can take to be (in the words of the Army) the best you can be. Whether you're striving to move up the corporate ladder, run your own company, or manage your household, the chapters keep you from making excuses for not achieving what you're capable of. The personal insights from Ivy show you how just about anything is possible as long as you work at it in the right way.

I wish I had this book when I began my career. I'm not sure I consciously took charge of my life because I never thought about it; I just acted. When I decided to go to law school in the 1970s, I never thought it was somewhat of a reach for a woman. When I became a volunteer firefighter in my town—the only woman in the company—it never occurred to me to ask whether this was an appropriate thing to do for a working mother. I just did it, and fortunately, the choices proved sound. I've raised strong, independent children, and I've built wonderful relationships with colleagues going back decades. I've garnered awards recognizing my books and blogs. I've continued to learn new things and take on new challenges. And I look forward to my work every day because I never know what new opportunities I'll encounter. Reflecting now on what I've done, I see that I followed the techniques and strategies that Ivy explains in the book. In particular, I've used the lessons on setting goals, networking, continually learning, conquering fears, creating a healthy lifestyle, and being persistent. I can particularly relate to Ivy's list-making, which is a habit we share. There are many more lessons in this book for you to think about and put into practice.

I've painted a rosy picture of my experiences, but I'd be remiss if I didn't add that there were also many failures and disappointments. There were challenges I couldn't overcome. There are always unexpected forces—a changing economy, illnesses, and even a pandemic (COVID-19)—that can derail your efforts. Having the information from this book in front of you can keep you on track.

When I taught a college course *Principles of Entrepreneurship,* I asked my students to define what they thought was success. As you may imagine, I got a wide range of answers, from making a lot of money and creating jobs to becoming a public corporation. Many had good ideas about how their businesses could help the environment or meet an important need in the marketplace. I challenged them to think about the bigger picture of their life, including how to achieve a work-life balance that could ultimately be viewed as a real success. Applying what you read in *Unleash Your Inner She-EO* can enable you to become the She-EO of your life and run things according to your plan.

Ivy loves quotations as you'll see in this book, and I do too. They are great motivators. I have some quotations taped to my monitor to remind me of important things. So, I'll close with a quotation from Ralph Waldo Emerson: "The only person you are destined to become is the person you decide to be."

—BARBARA WELTMAN

Attorney, Author

President of Big Ideas for Small Business

Named one of the Top 100 Small Business Influencers

Called "the guru of small business taxes" by *The Wall Street Journal*

UNLEASH YOUR INNER SHE-EO

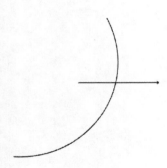

Introduction

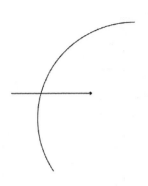

The Secret of Achieving Your Goals is to Get Started.

Every woman possesses the inherent ability to develop the necessary skills and mindset to embrace success, radiate confidence, and create a fulfilling and satisfying life. This journey involves adopting a CEO mindset and applying it to her personal and professional life. It doesn't matter whether or not a woman aspires to become a CEO of a business, she already holds the position of CEO of her household... and life.

In a world where success is often defined through the lens of traditional male standards, it's time for women to embrace their unique approach and navigate the path to success on their own terms. While many skills required for success are common to both genders, women bring distinct perspectives, strengths, and experiences to the table, allowing them to forge their own paths.

Within the pages of this book, I delve into various techniques and strategies to achieve and navigate success. I acknowledge that while certain traits may come naturally to men, they don't always come as easily to women. However, this is not a limitation, but an opportunity for growth and transformation. Women are not meant to do everything exactly like their male counterparts, but by thinking like a She-EO, we can accomplish all that we desire and turn our dreams into reality.

Throughout the course of this book, my intention is to inspire women to harness their unique strengths, perspectives, and aspirations to create their own definition of success. By adopting a She-EO mindset, I'm confident that women can achieve their every desire and transform their dreams into reality.

All CEOs share commonalities, but there are some significant differences in being a *female* CEO. As I reflect on my journey to building my company and achieving recognition as one of *INC Magazine's* fastest-growing private companies and a top solar company in the United States, I knew I couldn't follow the conventional path. The industry I was in was predominantly male-dominated, and I didn't fit into the traditional mold. Therefore, I had to create my own version of a roadmap that I could apply to any industry, any size of business, and any position in life. With the right beliefs and implementation of my success mindset, I was confident I would succeed.

Throughout my life, I've refined this process and mindset through trial and error, adapting to challenges, and enhancing my beliefs and methodologies. I firmly believe that by embracing the mentality of a She-EO, anyone can build the life they desire and dream of, both professionally and personally. It was also evident to me that true fulfillment for a woman entailed attaining success not only in her career but also in her personal life. Recognizing this, I felt compelled to write this book with the intention of helping as many women as possible in achieving both professional and personal success and fulfillment.

Before beginning, however, I felt it important to study other female CEO success stories. I began by researching statistics. I found that in 2023, forty-one women held CEO positions at S&P 500 companies. Fifty-two women made the Forbes' Fortune 500 list. To put that into perspective, that's 52 women out of approximately 169 million women in the United States. When I looked at the industry I was involved in, I found 24 female CEOs among the top 500 companies in America. These statistics intrigued me, especially because it appeared to me that millions of women were acting as CEOs in one manner or another.

Currently, there are approximately 13.94 million women-owned businesses in the United States according to the National Women's Business Council and the U.S. Census Bureau. However, it's important to consider the countless women who aspire to become a CEO, whether within an existing company or by building their own. Additionally, we are witnessing a surge in the creation of home-based businesses through platforms such as Etsy, Amazon, and eBay. These avenues, along with similar ones, have created opportunities for small businesses to emerge in every corner. I'd dare say that the actual number of small businesses and female CEOs is considerably higher than the reported 13.94 million.

Moreover, let's not overlook the women who effectively serve as CEOs of their households. I would estimate that this number far exceeds 25 million. In one way or another, most women need to possess the qualities of CEOs, whether for their professional endeavors or for managing their homes and lives successfully.

As I came to realize the significant number of women assuming the role of a CEO, I felt compelled to explore the essence of those three elusive letters – C.E.O., standing for Chief Executive Officer. Naturally, my initial question was about the literal meaning behind the acronym, but my curiosity extended further. What does it truly mean to be a CEO?

During my research, I found that ten areas of responsibility were often associated with the role of a CEO. These responsibilities make sure that the company:

1. Has a vision for the future.
2. Sets goals.
3. Provides the proper resources to achieve its goals.
4. Is financially responsible.
5. Grows and develops.

6. Maintains an awareness of companies that affect it.

7. Builds a corporate culture.

8. Makes good decisions.

9. Achieves its goals.

10. Is responsible for its results.

I believed that these responsibilities align perfectly with what we, as women, should strive to do for our own careers and lives. We should aim to:

1. Develop a vision for our future.

2. Set goals.

3. Provide proper resources to achieve our goals.

4. Be financially responsible.

5. Grow and develop.

6. Maintain awareness of those around us.

7. Build a personal culture to live by.

8. Make good decisions.

9. Achieve our goals.

10. Hold ourselves responsible for our results.

Regardless of whether you see yourself as the CEO of a Fortune 500 company, the CEO of a large or small business, or the CEO of your household, we are all CEOs of our lives. By implementing the concepts, beliefs, and mindset presented in this book, I'm confident you can accomplish any dream you have set for yourself. As women, we hold a responsibility to ourselves. Every woman needs to embrace her inner She-EO and manage her life as if it were a multi-million-dollar corporation.

Join me in a transformative journey as we explore practical strategies and insights into a mindset to help you unleash your inner She-EO. It's time to embrace your power and create a life that not only aligns with your ambition but also brings you unparalleled joy and fulfillment. Get ready to redefine success and embrace your inner She-EO.

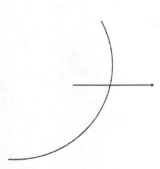

SELF-PERCEIVED
Limitations

Without Limitations, the Sky is the Limit.

"If we can see past preconceived limitations, then the possibilities are endless."

Amy Purdy

Growing up in a family of four girls, I never learned strong boundaries that dictated what a boy or girl should or could do. My upbringing was a beautiful blend of feminine and masculine experiences, where I learned a diverse range of skills. I was expected to embrace traditional "ladylike" activities such as cooking and sewing, but at the same time, I learned how to fish, catch snakes, and shoot a gun. My toys reflected this multifaceted upbringing as I cherished both my cuddly baby dolls and my big yellow Tonka truck that I could play with in the sandpile.

The world was my playground, and I eagerly immersed myself in adventures that knew no gender boundaries. I would roam the woods, climb trees, and build secret clubhouses, relishing the thrill of exploration. Simultaneously, I delighted in dressing up in extravagant evening gowns, indulging in make-believe scenarios while playing house with my dolls. One grandfather treated me like a princess, while the other treated me like a tom-boy. Their expectations were very different of me, but looking back,

I was fortunate to be exposed to such a variety of experiences, expectations… and lack of expectations.

In my family, the philosophy that was ingrained in me from an early age was that I could do anything with dedication and effort. This belief stemmed not only from a desire to empower us girls but also out of necessity. With no boys in the family, we all had to share the responsibilities and complete the necessary chores. The chores needed to be done, and we girls had to do them. There were no excuses. As an example: one grandfather called me Skinny-Minny due to being so thin and petite, yet I was still expected to carry and stack heavy bales of hay into the barn. Yes, it was more physically challenging for me to do this than it may have been for a larger boy, but I never backed down. I got the job done. Everyone had to help.

My upbringing also ingrained conflicting messages within me. On one hand, I was often told that as a girl, "I should be seen and not heard." On the other hand, my father emphasized repeatedly to me, "Be a leader, not a follower." These contrasting statements initially perplexed me, but as time passed, I learned how to weave them together and incorporate both aspects into my evolving personality. I discovered that I could assert myself confidently while also respecting and valuing my softer side.

However, the most valuable lesson I gained from my upbringing was the unwavering belief that my gender, size, or any other limitation I could think of was inconsequential in determining my potential. I learned that I could pursue my dreams and aspirations regardless of any perceived boundaries. **I could do just about anything I wanted if I put some effort into it.** This was how I was raised and how I've lived my life. It was never that I thought I was invincible and believed I could conquer anything effortlessly; instead, it was about cultivating a deep sense of belief. **I learned to believe in myself. If I wholeheartedly believed enough in what I wanted to do, set my mind to it, put in the effort, and dedicated myself to its pursuit, I knew I had the power to achieve it.**

Thus, my upbringing instilled within me a sense of limitless potential. It taught me to embrace my authentic self, free from societal expectations and constraints. I embarked on life's journey with an unwavering spirit, ready to conquer challenges, pursue my passions, and prove that the power of self-belief can propel us to extraordinary heights.

Did I become an overachiever? Absolutely.

Am I still? Yes and no.

Work is my passion. Challenges invigorate me, and keeping my mind engaged and active brings me immense joy. Some might label me as a workaholic, but I believe I have crafted a well-rounded and balanced life.

Despite the time and effort I dedicate to business, I make it a priority to indulge in the pleasures of life. I carve out moments for exhilarating tennis matches with friends, quality time with my beloved family, enriching travels, and the catharsis of writing. Somehow, amidst it all, I manage to fit everything in, retiring to bed early most evenings and rising at the crack of dawn.

Many people have been surprised by my success. How did a seemingly unassuming, introverted woman like me ascend to the position of chief financial officer in a white-collar public company listed on NASDAQ, retire in my late thirties, and subsequently become the chief executive officer of a completely different blue-collar enterprise in which I initially possessed no expertise? The curiosity surrounding my journey is what inspired me to pen this book. I wanted to share the invaluable lessons I learned throughout my life—lessons that propelled me forward and enabled me to accomplish my goals. Although not every step came effortlessly, and many presented immense challenges, I persevered because these achievements were essential to me, and I refused to succumb to self-imposed limitations.

Every day, I actively strive to manifest the life I desire. It is a deliberate and conscious effort. To embark on your transformative journey toward realizing the life you yearn for, I offer you a vital starting point:

Embrace a mindset where you don't create any self-imposed limitations regarding anything you do.

A person can create thousands of mental limitations. For example:

- I can't own a business – Why? I'm not smart enough... or I don't have a college degree... or I don't know how...

- I can't earn $100,000 a year – Why? Because no one in my family ever earned that much ... or no one would pay me that kind of money... or there is nothing I could do that would be worth that...

- I can never attract a good man in my life – Why? I'm not pretty enough... or I always pick losers... I'm too old, and all the men I meet like younger women...

The moment a limitation is believed by you, it becomes real whether it is or not. Limitations will stop you from succeeding.

Allow yourself the opportunity to TRY!

The first step to overcoming a limiting belief is to realize you may have one! If you find that you have a limiting belief, make it a habit to write it down. Personally, I keep a hard-cover, 5x8 lined journal where I record my goals, strategies of how to achieve them, beliefs – both positive and limiting, thoughts, and other notes that I feel are important. I also like to highlight everything I've accomplished. This practice allows me to revisit my progress and see how much I've achieved. There is an immense sense of satisfaction, encouragement, and motivation from seeing page after page highlighted in yellow!

As an avid list-maker, I have discovered the incredible value of organizing information in a concise and structured manner. Lists offer me clarity, readability, and enhanced retention. Furthermore, their flexibility allows me to adapt and refine my thoughts as I progress. If I come across a bullet point that fails to resonate with me positively, I gladly rewrite it to reflect something that does.

For example, I write a thought down. It can be any thought I have. It can even be negative such as *I'm too old to start a new business*. Realizing this is a negative and self-limiting belief, I'll then write a new statement directly below it that is more positive such as, *I can start a new business at any age*.

Then I add the reasons *why* this could be a true statement.

I can start a new business at any age because:
- *I have more experience now than I did when I was younger.*

- *I have a clear vision of what I want to achieve.*

- *I'm focused and have the time to dedicate to the business.*

- *I am in a good financial position to do this at this stage in my life.*

- *I have a bigger network of people who can help, etc.*

With lists as my trusty tool, I navigate through life's complexities with more ease, clarity, and intention.

When you write things down, it's easy to see a negative or limiting statement and then change it to something more affirming. What you say and what you think, however, is much more difficult to recognize and correct. Frankly, it's easy for limiting statements to be verbalized. We've all done it, and most likely will do it again in the future. But what is of most concern to me, is that in one year's time, I hear more limiting beliefs from women than I have heard in my lifetime from men. I think, for the most part, women state their limiting thoughts because they believe it's unflattering to toot their own horn or be confident in their abilities. Instead, many downplay their accomplishments and either don't discuss them or temper them with negative statements.

I recall a luncheon with friends shortly after the new year began. The topic of New Year's resolutions came up. One friend stated she didn't write resolutions and quickly followed up with the statement: "It's probably why I'm not as successful as all of you!" Another friend chimed in that her goal was, "To lose twenty pounds... because I'm so fat." Another friend hesitantly responded that her goal was to finally quit her management job and open her own consulting firm. Yet, to follow suit, she immediately negated the statement. Whether to conform to the other's presentations or to verbalize her own limiting thought, she followed up with, "But this will probably be a huge mistake."

Of course, in each of these situations, everyone encouraged the others and recapped all their positive, successful attributes. So, when the time came for me to expose one of my resolutions, I thought for a minute. Am I looking for outward affirmation, or do I have a limiting thought about my resolution? To be honest, I did have a limiting belief. I had set a very lofty goal and wasn't sure I would achieve it, but I didn't want to verbalize that. As a result, I consciously had to think how exactly I would word my resolution so as not to sound limiting or negative. It was tough. I could have easily fallen into the same trap as my friends – who by the way are all beautiful, successful, and brilliant in their own way. Yet, this showed me how easy it is to state self-limiting or negative statements toward oneself.

Pay close attention to the language you use. Take a moment to truly listen to the words you speak to others and yourself regarding your beliefs. Are you inadvertently reinforcing and perpetuating your own limiting beliefs in conversations? Are you openly sharing these beliefs with others, offering explanations and excuses as to why you hold them and why success seems unattainable? Recognizing the power of your words and the impact they have on your mindset is essential to transforming your beliefs and embracing a path to success.

Check your thoughts and language at the door and make sure they are both positive, even if they may not be 100% true now. **Every thought, no matter how seemingly insignificant, can create a ripple effect.** Consciously choosing to speak and think in a manner that is fully supportive of you and your goals will pave the way for accelerated progress toward your dreams.

The third step is to **stop identifying yourself with self-limiting beliefs.** Many limiting beliefs may have been with you since childhood through no fault of your own. Possibly you were a little chubby as a child and were told that you have fat genes like your Aunt Mary. Poor obese Aunt Mary's image will forever be in your thoughts whenever you eat or look in the mirror. But maybe Aunt Mary simply didn't have good eating habits, sat on the couch daily watching soaps, didn't exercise, or had a genetic disorder. Who knows? All I know is that YOU aren't AUNT MARY! So, get her out of your head! Create a new belief. A simple statement such as, *I feel healthy and great,* may be all you need. The more you reiterate this to yourself, the more likely you will take steps toward making it become a reality. Think about joining a gym, taking a walk around the block each night, or cutting one dessert out a week. Whatever you do, STOP seeing yourself as Aunt Mary!

Finally, take one small step to prove the limiting belief wrong. Challenge yourself to step forward and put this belief behind you and create a new belief in its place. As an example, possibly you'd love to write a book, but your limiting belief is that you don't have time. Analyze your time and find thirty minutes a day to write. It could be during your lunch hour, by getting up thirty minutes earlier, or by giving up watching thirty minutes of television at night. Once you prove to yourself that you can make the time for things that matter to you, this belief will slowly dissipate.

By recognizing you have a limiting belief and taking the above steps toward changing it, you will quickly put it behind you. This pivotal moment unleashes a world of opportunities that previously may have seemed daunting. Whatever your aspirations may be, hold a firm belief that you can achieve them. Take decisive actions toward your goals, and I have no doubt that you will achieve resounding success.

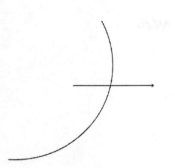

DEVELOP A
VISION FOR YOUR

Create a Compelling
Vision of a Life
You're Excited to Live.

"Create a vision for the life you really want, and then work relentlessly toward making it a reality."

Roy T. Bennett

Do you recall as a child hearing your friends say when they grew up, they were going to be a teacher, a doctor, or maybe even an astronaut? Maybe they even had the specificity of saying they wanted to be married with three children and live in a blue house with a white picket fence. Their innocent visions of the future allowed them to visualize themselves as someone they presently did not know themselves to be.

Then, in high school, we were asked, "What do you want to do when you graduate?" We all thought for a moment, and most of us decided on one of two choices: go to college or go to work immediately after graduating. *That was simple*, we thought. But the questioning didn't stop there. We were pressed for details. We were asked to determine not only what we wanted to *do*, but what we wanted to *be!* Some breezed through this question with determination in their voice stating their dream of becoming a lawyer, business owner, or professional athlete. But when it came to me, I thought, *yikes! This is real.* Yes, I wanted to go to college, but for what? I had no idea.

I felt overwhelmed, so I took several aptitude tests to try and gain some clarity, but even then, I found myself torn between different fields of study: an architect (because I was a decent artist), an ophthalmologist (because there was only one in town, and I figured he was getting old and I could take over his business), an accountant (because I had won a state competition in the field and it came easily), or an insurance agent (because it was an industry my father was in.) *There,* I thought. *I've narrowed it down.* Yet, when I gave this information to my guidance counselor, I was told I had chosen four very different fields of study – one creative, one medical, one business, and one in sales. I was all over the board, and I had no idea what to do, and it stressed me out terribly. I ultimately chose business as a field of study when I realized that I didn't have to know *what* I wanted to be… I just had to know *what field* I wanted to be in. That was the first time I had to seriously start developing a vision for my life.

After college and as the years went on, I found that **my vision for my life and future could change.** Priorities shifted, and as new opportunities emerged, things that were once important no longer held any importance. Things I never considered even a few years prior, were now exciting and significant. I quickly learned that **establishing a vision for my life was not a one-time event** like I had thought it was back in school. **It was a continuous, and ever-evolving process.**

Regardless of how my vision changed, however, two constants remained: First, my life had to have meaning. I believe we are all here for a reason, therefore, there must be a purpose. Second, my life had to inspire me and keep me motivated to work toward it. With these guiding principles as my foundation, I then began to paint a picture of my future in my mind. I visualized myself as having whatever I wanted and doing whatever I wanted to do, and I allowed my mind to dream without limitation. I thought of it as time traveling. With my imagination, I got to create my ideal life and act as if it were real. With these visions, it allowed me to determine who I wanted to be, what I wanted to do, who I wanted in my life, and the primary purpose that would guide it.

Surprisingly, many people never take the time to envision a different life for themselves from where they are at present. Instead, they fall into the dogmatic pattern of drifting through their days, allowing external circumstances to dictate their life instead of creating them on purpose. The monotonous routine of work, socializing, and daily activities becomes their reality.

Get up.

Get Dressed.

Go to work.

Meet friends after work.

Have a few drinks.

Eat something.

Go to bed.

Repeat.

Over time, these individuals are seduced into a limited and clouded version of their life. They become complacent, failing to see the importance of visualizing anything different than what extends beyond their current circumstances. Their days aren't *that bad*, and they don't recognize the monotony that has enveloped them. It's often not until a jarring event such as the loss of a job, a divorce, or simply an overwhelming feeling of unhappiness or discontent before they recognize the hamster wheel they've been on. In the aftermath, they grapple with a profound amount of regret, mourning for time squandered and missed opportunities. At this point, a yearning for change can arise, but the pressing question looms large: What now?

When you are ready to envision a different future for yourself, there are steps to take that will help you along the way. First, **don't overthink with your head.** Think from your heart and create a vision that overwhelms you with gratitude. You should visualize a life that you would be so thankful for, you can feel it in your heart. You can always create goals later that help you to get there, but first try to **see, feel, hear, and taste your dream with no limitations.**

As Robert Fritz stated, "If you limit your choices only to what seems possible or reasonable, you disconnect yourself from what you truly want, and all that is left is a compromise."

Before you begin to develop a vision for your future, let go of rational thinking and step outside the confines of your comfort zone. Imagine you have a magic wand, and when you wave it, it will create everything you've ever imagined for yourself no matter how far-fetched it may seem to your rational mind. Visualize your ideal life in all the excess and glory that you want. Imagine details that bring you satisfaction, happiness, and fulfillment, and engage all your senses to dream without limitations.

While doing this, keep in mind a quote by Khalil Gibran. "We are limited, not by our abilities, but by our vision." **Don't limit yourself.**

Use some of the following questions to help you develop a vision of your future.

1. Know who you are at your core.
    1. What are your values?
    2. What is important to you?
    3. What inspires you?
    4. What are you passionate about?

2. Identify your gifts and strengths.

    1. What are your strengths?

    2. What are your natural talents?

    3. What is your best personality trait?

    4. What sets you apart from others?

3. Envision how you want to live your life.

    1. Where are you living?

    2. Who are you with?

    3. How do you feel?

    4. What is your ideal day like?

The goal is to get lost in the details and imagine all that you can while not limiting yourself. It's time to remember how to play "make-believe". Though it may seem foolish at first to think of yourself as having no financial worries, sharing a nice home with someone you love, and having a job that you're excited to go to each day, it's the first step in the great formula for achievement, happiness, and success. **When you pretend something is possible, it's the first building block to creating the future you desire.** If you can envision a different life and believe it's possible, then you can begin on goals to work to create it. Several successful people have similar ways of saying this:

Napoleon Hill: "Whatever the mind of man can conceive, and believe, it can achieve."

Walt Disney: "If you can dream it, you can do it."

Eleanor Roosevelt: "The future belongs to those who believe in the beauty of their dreams."

Muhammad Ali: "If my mind can conceive it, and my heart can believe it, then I can achieve it."

Arnold Schwarzenegger: "If I can see it and believe it, then I can achieve it."

It's interesting to see how these quotes from different individuals all revolve around the concept of the power of belief, visualization, and determination in achieving one's goals. While the wording might differ slightly, the underlying message remains consistent: believing in your dreams and visualizing success are essential factors in turning aspirations into reality. These quotes have become motivational mantras for many people seeking inspiration and encouragement to create the life they desire and achieve their ambitions.

Determine your ideal version of your life, visualize it, and then let it begin to guide you in everything you do going forward. The more you practice envisioning this future, the more you will begin to believe it has the potential to be possible. As Christopher Reeve declared, "So many of our dreams seem impossible, then improbable, then inevitable." **Believe in your dreams so much that they become inevitable.**

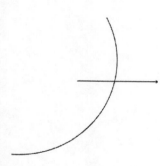

BELIEVE IN *Yourself*

Believe in Yourself and Become Unstoppable.

"Follow your dreams, believe in yourself,
and don't give up."

Rachel Corrie

Though I graduated from high school at the top of my class, when it was time to meet with my guidance counselor, to my astonishment, he suggested that I forgo college and instead just get married and have kids. Granted, I did get engaged during my senior year (which in retrospect wasn't a smart thing to do). Still, his comments rubbed me the wrong way and deeply offended me. How dare he try to limit me or push his beliefs on me that I shouldn't go to college. I was far from unintelligent. I made the National Honor Society, was in Student Council, was a class officer, and ... I was a *leader, not a follower!* I had plans for my life, and not pursuing higher education was certainly not part of my plan. This counselor confined me to the role of homemaker, dutifully massaging someone's feet upon their return from work! No way!

As you can guess, this more than riled me up. I have numerous friends who are wonderful homemakers and love that life, but it just wasn't the life I saw for myself. I had been working since I was thirteen years old doing one thing or another. I worked two jobs my senior year and loved every minute of it. So, without his support, I enlisted the help of my employer, and he helped me pull together college applications. If I had let my guidance counselor's beliefs become mine, I might never have pursued a college degree.

It's critical to **never let someone else's beliefs about you become your reality, never let someone else determine your future, and never let someone else determine your belief in yourself.**

It could have been very easy for me to agree with this counselor since I *was* getting married after high school. I could have easily thought, *yes, he's right. I need to be a good wife and not worry about going to college. I can always get some sort of job.* This man simply saw me as a young girl who was engaged and getting married at eighteen. His guidance may have been due to his previous experience, from guiding other eighteen-year-old girls for the past twenty years and statistics based on them. His comments may have had nothing to do with me at all. Who knows, and who cares! These were his beliefs, and they had nothing to do with me or my future. I'm sure you've heard the adage, **"What others think of you is none of your business."** There is truth in that statement. What you think of yourself is the only thing that holds any importance.

Throughout my life, I have witnessed numerous instances where individuals owned the narrative of someone else's opinion of them.

Thankfully, I've also seen where another's opinion was rejected, and self-belief prevailed. I met a successful, but unhappy man who went into farming simply because his entire family had been farmers for generations. He was miserable and always wanted to be a stockbroker, but his family told him that he could never do that because he didn't go to college, wasn't smart enough, and only knew how to farm. After many conversations, along with an opportunity to work for a brokerage firm, he defied his family and left behind the comfort of what he knew and their beliefs in who he was, to become a successful stockbroker. Unfortunately, however, this man carried around others' beliefs about himself for almost forty years before taking a chance in believing in himself. He's one of the lucky ones, though, as many people carry others' beliefs with them for all their lives.

Who have you believed in throughout your life? Maybe your parents? Your spouse? A boss, or a child? When you believe in someone else, your emotions and feelings run high, and you have confidence that this person will make the right decisions, attempt to succeed, or do the best he or she can do. But ultimately, does it really matter that you believed in them? Maybe. Maybe not, except for the fact that it may have helped them believe in themselves. We can encourage, support, and love, which are all beautiful acts and sentiments to be the recipient of, but without the recipient having those same beliefs for themselves, it may not matter.

As an example: Becky loved basketball, and tryouts for the team were coming up. Her mother and father encouraged her, believed in her, and were confident she'd make the team. They watched as she shot hoops for hours in the backyard. Daily, her father ran drills with her to help her to be a quicker and better player. Then tryouts came. On the court, she blew all her free throws, tripped dribbling, and lost the ball to other players each time she had it. She didn't make the team. What happened? Becky didn't believe she fit in. She knew she was a good ballplayer, but the other girls were all part of a certain clique in school that Becky wasn't part of. She thought they were better players, prettier, and more popular than she was. She didn't believe she belonged on *their* team. So, unconsciously she sabotaged herself. Without self-belief, it didn't matter her skill level. She was sure that she didn't belong with them or on *their* team.

However, Natalie was a bit less skilled than many of the basketball players. Yet, despite these shortcomings, when she went to the tryouts for the team, her enthusiasm ran high, she was positive, she worked harder than the rest, and gave 110% because she believed she would make the team. The coach was on the fence about her. After the tryouts, he asked her why she believed she should make the team. Natalie stated with confidence that she believed she would be a great teammate, would lead by example of hard work and dedication, and knew she would end up being one of the coach's best players! The coach immediately added her to the roster.

Belief in oneself serves as the cornerstone of our journey. Without it, we often exclude ourselves before we have a chance to belong. Often, we refrain from trying due to the fear of failure. We harbor self-doubt, depriving ourselves of the possibility of aspiring for greater things. We are quick to compare ourselves to others, and often automatically give ourselves the self-imposed short stick! Without self-belief, we remain distant from unlocking our true potential.

As our self-beliefs strengthen, our doubts and fears diminish, and our confidence grows. We become more willing to take risks and pursue our deepest desires. Our attention shifts toward the positive, emphasizing our strengths and nurturing the expectation of attaining our goals. While success may not always be guaranteed, it's never due to a lack of effort. We give it our all and commit ourselves to every endeavor; and regardless of the outcome, our willingness to try sets us apart, ensuring that we achieve more than we would have without this effort.

A powerful approach to enhancing self-belief is acknowledging and celebrating the accomplishments that you have already achieved. Pull out your journal and write a list of things that you've accomplished and achieved in your life so far. Examples may be: You graduated summa kum laude. You've met your weight goal. You recently got a promotion at work. You've raised two wonderful children. Then write a list of everything you feel you *excel* at. Examples may be: You're very creative. You make great cookies. You're a wonderful listener. You're a good problem solver, etc. The more you can list, the more your confidence and belief in yourself will grow.

Then at the end of each day, reflect on your day's interactions, the positive things that happened, how you handled difficult situations, and what you accomplished. Find a couple of key situations where you felt you did a great job and jot these down in your journal as well. Self-reflection is essential to personal growth, which fosters a stronger sense of self-belief.

Norman Vincent Peale, who is considered the father of positive thinking stated, "Believe in yourself! Have faith in your abilities! Without a humble, but reasonable confidence in your own powers, you cannot be successful or happy."

Magic happens when you believe in yourself, and ultimately, it's a critical key to a successful life. **Once you have *YOU* on your side, that's the beginning of the magic.**

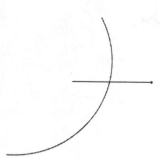

CREATE DESIRE AND
Motivation

Desire is the Driving Force of Motivation.

"Desire is the key to motivation."

Tony Robbins

I don't care how intelligent someone is, if they aren't *motivated*, they most likely won't succeed in their endeavors. And if they don't possess *desire* toward their goals, they most likely won't find the motivation necessary to achieve them.

Desire and motivation are two powerful forces that can propel us to achieve great things. **They are intertwined forces that have the potential to drive us toward success;** but without them, even the most intelligent individual may fall short. While intelligence is undoubtedly valuable, it's not the sole determinant of success. Intelligence can provide the tools, knowledge, and skills necessary for achievement, but history is filled with examples of those who achieved extraordinary feats despite not being exceptionally intellectually gifted. Their success stemmed from their passion and determination which pushed them to surpass all expectations.

Desire, in its essence, represents a longing, a passion, or an intense feeling for something. It surpasses mere wants and extends into a deeper realm of longing. While a want may be to enjoy a nice meal at your favorite restaurant, a desire goes beyond that, such as wanting to share that meal with someone special. Wants are often temporary, whereas desires typically last much longer.

Desires are often the driving force that ignites the spark within us and urges us to pursue our dreams. They provide the emotional connection and significance necessary to fuel our efforts. Without desire, goals remain merely ideas that lack the emotional connection needed to drive the effort to pursue them or give them significance. Desires have the power to evoke a sense of purpose, passion, and determination. They give meaning to our pursuits and are often connected to our core values, beliefs, and personal identity.

Motivation, on the other hand, is the force that compels us to take action to achieve our goals. It pushes us to overcome challenges and persevere in the direction of success. Without it, our desires can remain like idle wishes, lacking the drive to transform them into reality.

It's important to recognize that **desire and motivation are deeply personal and subjective experiences.** What ignites the flame of desire in one person may be entirely different from what resonates with another. Similarly, the factors that drive motivation can vary greatly from individual to individual.

Athletes Serena Williams and Usain Bolt demonstrate this principle. Williams, arguably the greatest female tennis player of all time, was driven by the love of the game, the thrill of competition, and the desire to continually improve her skills. Her motivation and passion propelled her to become the best female tennis players in the world. Usain Bolt, considered the greatest sprinter of all time, was motivated by the exhilaration of running at record-breaking speeds and pushing the limits of human performance. While both athletes were passionate about their sports, their specific motivations differed.

I know two very successful and financially wealthy individuals. When I asked about the factors behind the first person's success, she shared that she had grown up in poverty with an abusive father who always belittled her and insisted she was worthless. Her burning desire to prove him wrong was a powerful motivator for success. This desire fueled her motivation to build a successful business in hopes her father would finally say he was proud of her and tell her that she did a great job. Those words were never uttered despite her success; but she has since forgiven her father and thanked him for igniting within her such a strong desire, which ultimately resulted in the achievement of her goals.

The second individual's story was similar as she grew up in like circumstances, but her burning desire was her unwavering determination to never find herself reliant on anyone else for food, shelter, or support.

She was driven to be in control of her life and shield herself from the hardships of poverty and abuse. Through sheer diligence, she built a prominent law firm where she was able to help others who were faced with similar adversities. Her success grew quickly from her initial desire, which fueled her motivation to achieve success.

Whatever your desires are, it's essential to nurture and cultivate them. Take time to reflect on what truly matters to you, identify your passions, and use this information to strengthen them.

When you align desire with motivation, you are more likely to achieve your goal. However, when those two are misaligned, you might find yourself feeling frustrated and discouraged. Your desire may be strong, but if your motivation is weak, results will not be produced as you'd like. Set meaningful and achievable goals based on your desires that create a strong sense of purpose – serving as a constant reminder of why you embarked on this journey in the first place.

A simple and common example illustrates this point. When my college friends and I were nearing graduation, we discussed our plans for securing jobs. Our common desire was to have employment lined up immediately after graduation. Those of us who were passionate and committed to this desire immediately felt motivated to act. I wrote and printed multiple copies of my resume and began visiting businesses in my desired field. I introduced myself, submitted my resume, and followed up weekly until I received a job offer. Some of my friends were surprised by how quickly I had secured a position while they still had no prospects. They possessed one component, desire, but didn't possess the motivation to act until well after graduation.

Recognizing and nurturing your desires is a transformative journey that leads to profound personal growth and self-awareness. It requires delving deep into your innermost thoughts and feelings, allowing you to understand what truly resonates with your heart and soul. This process of introspection not only helps you to identify your passions and desires but also unveils the underlying values and beliefs that drive them. By being attuned to your authentic desires, you gain a compass that guides you toward a life filled with purpose and meaning.

Once you have unraveled your deepest desires, the next crucial step is to align them with action. This alignment bridges the gap between mere wishful thinking and concrete progress. It infuses you with a renewed sense of determination and vigor and a wellspring of motivation that propels you forward on your chosen path. The synergy between your desires, motivation, and actions ignites a powerful force within you, enabling you to move forward toward your desires. You become the architect of your destiny, actively shaping your life in a way that feels fulfilling and purposeful.

While desire is the catalyst for transformation and achievement, it's through motivation that it becomes the relentless pursuit of dreams. With each step you take, you progress, you learn to adapt, you grow, and you continuously refine your approach to move you one step closer to your dreams. The journey may be challenging, but the fulfillment that comes from witnessing your desires materialize into reality is unparalleled. Embracing the harmony that desire and motivation share unlocks the full potential of what we can achieve and experience in life.

The quote, "Intense, burning desire is the motivational force that enables you to overcome any obstacle and achieve almost any goal," encapsulates the incredible power of unwavering desire, motivation, and determination. When you possess an intense and burning desire to achieve something, it becomes the driving force that propels you forward to reach it.

DETERMINE YOUR

Value

Confidence Comes From Knowing Your Value.

"If you don't know your own value, someone will tell you your value, and it will be less than you're worth."

Bernard Hopkins

When I graduated from college, I went to work for a stock brokerage and insurance firm. I was hired as a secretary-bookkeeper, and I started at $4 an hour – which was a whopping $8,320 a year! Cha-Ching! I thought I had made it to the big leagues. After all, the minimum wage at that time was $3.35, so I was thrilled. That is, however, until I started doing payroll for the company and saw some people making $50,000 - $75,000+ a year! What was the difference? I was an employee of the company, and I **let someone else determine my value.** They hired me and said, "Your position and YOU are valued at $8,000 to us." The people who were earning $50,000-$75,000+ a year **determined their own value.** They were agents, advisors, and brokers and took no salary or hourly wage. Instead, they were commission-based only, and they were paid based on the business they brought to the company. The company didn't dictate their value. These brokers and advisors determined their own value based on their actions.

Though I loved every aspect of my job, I wanted more. So, in my spare time (which wasn't much between work and family) I studied to obtain all the licenses necessary to do what the brokers and advisors did. During work hours I listened... watched... and learned from all the successful men. Did I just say "men"? Yes, there were only male brokers and advisors back then. Thankfully, they were happy to share their knowledge with me because the more I knew, the more I could assist them. I'd help them with their clients, paperwork, monitoring portfolios, or whatever else was needed. The more I learned, the more I wanted to learn, and the more valuable I became to the firm.

Even though everyone in sales was male, and even though everyone earning the higher income was male....

- I could envision myself doing what they were doing.

- I didn't have any limitations that said I **couldn't** do it. No one said a woman couldn't be a broker, a financial advisor, or an insurance agent and earn $50,000 a year. There was just no one doing it that I knew of!

- I believed in myself and knew that if these men could do it, so could I. I didn't think they were any more intelligent or any more deserving. I had belief in myself.

- Finally, I didn't have any fear. There was no fear of change, or fear that I'd fail. Fear could have stopped me immediately, and I could have come up with thousands of fear-based excuses to hold me back, but I didn't.

By the age of 27, I was ready. I was fully licensed and all set to step out on a limb and become a full-time financial advisor. But then I learned that I was pregnant with my second child. The advisors in the firm didn't work 9-5. Most of their work took place from 6 pm–10 pm because that was the only time they could meet with the breadwinners of families – after they had finished their work for the day. I didn't want to take my evenings away from my son and newborn, so after careful consideration, I thought it best to put my plan on the back burner. I chose to focus on my children and family while continuing to work in the office.

Many might assume that I didn't achieve my goal of determining my value, but I did. During that significant period, I recognized that my value lay in being there for my family. My time held greater worth when spent with them. This is a sentiment that resonates with many women. It is easy to advocate for pursuing your aspirations without hesitation, but for women, it is rarely that straightforward. It is not a matter of choosing between a career or family; it is about embracing both and finding the delicate balance that works best.

I'd love to say that I jumped in with both feet and was an immediate and huge success. I didn't, however, and I have no regrets about how I spent those couple of years. **Personal values cannot be measured by a price tag,** and by remaining true to what mattered most to me, I was able to **know my value** as well as **respect my worth.**

When I say *Determine Your Value* at the beginning of this chapter, understand that two aspects allow you to do this. There is a financial aspect and a personal aspect. I did eventually become a financial advisor, and I far exceeded my expectations, goals, and financial objectives. I knew what I was *worth* financially, and I took the steps necessary to prove it and achieve it. Yet, I also knew my *personal value*. While both financial worth and personal value are important and go together, they are also very different. My *value* to my children, family, and household had tremendous importance to me, therefore it was my number one priority. This was where I felt I could contribute the most value and where I was worth more than money. I also understood what my financial worth would be to the company while I continued to only do the tasks of my existing job.

When I chose family, I didn't choose to pursue my career as a full-time financial advisor at that time. So, by saying yes to one thing, I said no to something else. The decision I made had benefits but also opportunity costs. While I'd like to say you can have it all, sometimes you can't. Those who tell you that you can, may be blind to the costs. There are opportunity costs to every decision made. But if we try to be everything to everyone and be fully committed to every possibility, we may end up busy, but not true to ourselves.

It wasn't until a year and a half after my second child was born that I figured out how to modify my current job situation to include meeting and advising clients during my chosen working hours. It also wasn't how I first envisioned the transition into this career. Originally, I thought it was an all-or-nothing deal – one or the other. Family versus work, and even advising clients versus my current position as an accounting/sales assistant. Also, I had originally thought I had to practice the career like the male advisors did – in the evening hours. I was lucky enough and smart enough to figure out how to rearrange and streamline my existing job and incorporate all appointments with clients into my 9-5 working hours. You know the saying: *build it, and they will come.* Well, they did, and within my schedule, which still left me time with my family. This became a win-win for me and for the company, and in the first year of this hybrid-job situation I made well more than my $50,000 goal.

When assessing your personal value, it's crucial to identify what holds the most importance to you. If you find yourself comparing different situations, you can evaluate them based on your priorities. However, it's important to note that your choices may not be like mine where I prioritized dedicating more time to family over immediate business goals. You may find yourself deciding between two different positions, two companies to work for, or contemplating whether to work for someone else or start your own business. It could also revolve around choosing between part-time or full-time work, among numerous other possibilities we often encounter. In some cases, it might even involve deciding whether to remain in a relationship or move on.

Regardless of the situation, take into consideration your likes and dislikes, what brings you the most joy, and where you believe you'll find the most happiness and sense of value. Once you understand these factors, you can begin to analyze the opportunity costs. If you're comfortable with the potential consequences, then you can confidently assert that you've made a sound decision. Embrace your choice and recognize **that you have just determined your own value.**

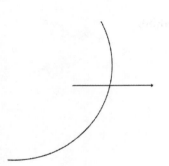

MANAGE YOUR
Time

Time is a Precious Resource. Make Every Minute Count.

"Time = Life; therefore, waste your time and waste your life, or master your time and master your life."

Alan Lakein

At any given moment, you can reflect upon your life and recognize that **your present situation is a direct result of your past decisions.** Each day presents you with the profound ability to shape your future through the choices you make regarding how you invest your time. Dismissing the significance of your time would be a huge misconception, for the truth remains that **what you choose to do today holds the power to enhance or diminish your future tomorrow.**

When I finally decided I was ready to become a financial advisor, I knew the time was right. I was excited at the potential opportunity of advising someone, but I found myself even more passionate about helping other women gain financial knowledge to plan for their future security. Regardless of whether I acquired clients or not, my primary objective in undertaking this transition was simply to help women. To accomplish this, I knew the most effective means of reaching a wide audience would be through a book. Undoubtedly, I possessed a wealth of knowledge and unwavering belief in the ideas I wished to convey. However, I was also aware that writing a book would demand a substantial amount of time and effort.

I understood that dedicating my time at present had the potential to benefit a greater number of women in the future. Looking at my life, however, I worked full-time and had a family with two children. My children were extremely active in sports and school activities, which took up most evenings and weekends. Also, we had two homes that I had to keep up, one being on a lake and over an hour away. Most weekends were full of packing, cleaning, shopping, and preparing to go back and forth. Where would I find the time to write? But it was important to me, so I knew I had to make the time.

After evaluating my schedule, I realized that once the children were in bed for the night and chores were done, I'd sit down and relax in front of the television from about nine to eleven. So, for the next sixty days, I gave up television and devoted that time to writing. I was amazed that I didn't miss TV, how energized I was each evening, and how quickly I had written my first book – a short, easy-to-understand book for women, *Women's Financial Wisdom – How to Become a Woman of Wealth*. Within just a short period after, it was picked up and published by a New York publishing house, and soon, I had my first book in my hands.

I received several positive reviews of the book, and then a nationwide publication, *Bottom Line Personal,* recommended it to its readers. As a result, book sales exploded, and speaking requests began to pour in. I had never done any public speaking before, and statistics say that 76% of the population has some sort of public speaking anxiety or phobia. I didn't focus on that. Instead, I prepared a twenty-minute talk and started accepting offers.

I began by speaking at small gatherings of women's groups across the state. Before long, my speaking engagements expanded to include prominent conferences, where I had the privilege of addressing audiences of hundreds of women at a time. This exposure led to invitations pouring in from various sources, including television appearances, all recognizing me as an authority on women and investing. It was gratifying to witness the realization of my passion for empowering women, and as a result, my clientele grew to a point where I found myself unable to accommodate everyone. The joy I experienced from pursuing a fulfilling vocation while making a significant impact on the lives of these women was unparalleled. I had attained my aspiration of becoming a successful financial advisor.

This is just one example of how my time each day affected my future. I'm certain you, too, could think of numerous examples in your own life. While you may feel you are very good about choosing how you spend your time, you may be shocked at how you inadvertently allow time to slip away without purpose.

We've all heard the quote, "Don't put off what you can do today until tomorrow." Yet regrettably, many fail to heed this advice. Uttering the words, "I'll do that tomorrow," is so easy to say and do. What's even more concerning is that we often trick ourselves into genuinely believing that we will indeed accomplish the task the following day! Then tomorrow becomes the next day, and then the next. "I'll start my diet tomorrow," is something I'm sure you've either heard or said. Day by day drifts by, and soon you are in a position where you have twenty pounds to lose versus ten.

Procrastination is a silent killer of your dreams. It lulls you into stagnant habits of stalling, deferring, and postponing. As a result, it stifles your progress and keeps you in a holding pattern that won't allow forward movement. **Today does affect your tomorrow no matter how you look at it. Your past will eventually catch up to you.**

If you don't **purposefully plan to make time to work on your life and your goals, you'll find you won't have the time.** Life gets busy, distractions happen, and time disappears like black matter in a vortex. Before you know it, time has slipped away and is gone forever.

The biggest complaint I hear about time, however, is that: "I don't have any time!" Though you've probably heard this before as well, I'll recount the facts about time.

There are 8,760 hours in a year.

According to statistics, per year most people:

- Work (including drive time) 2,340 hours (45 hours a week x 52 weeks)
- Sleep an average of 2,920 hours (8 hours a day)
- Spend 766 hours caring for or dedicating time with children. (2.1 hours a day)
- Spend 730 hours eating and on daily hygiene/exercise (2 hours a day)
- Spend 730 hours on social media (2 hours a day)
- Spend 1,825 watching TV or playing video games (5 hours a day)

You may look at these numbers and say there is no way most people spend five hours a day watching TV or playing video games; but yes, studies do show that the average person spends five hours and four minutes daily!

Also, when you add these numbers up, it equates to 9,311 hours versus 8,760 hours. This accounts for 1.5 hours daily as a variance, as not everyone does each of these things every day. Maybe you only spend two to three hours each night watching television and on social media. The point I want to make with this is simply that, as Americans, we are spending almost five hours more each day watching television and on social media than caring for our children. If that doesn't put things in perspective, I'm not sure what would. If we simply cut back a little TV or social media time, we may find the extra time we are looking for to spend with family, move up in our careers, build a business, and improve our current circumstances.

When you say you don't have enough time, keep in mind that you have the same hours per day as Michelangelo, Leonard da Vinci, Mozart, Helen Keller, Marie Curie, Louisa May Alcott, Albert Einstein, and everyone else. **We always have enough time.** We just need to **choose to use time to our advantage.**

John F. Kennedy once said, "We must use time as a tool, not as a couch." How many of us find ourselves spending our time on the couch? We watch sitcoms, reality shows, movies, and binge-watch Netflix series. For many years I gave up television altogether, and I must admit, I never missed it. Recently, however, I began watching a few Netflix shows, and I'm disturbed at how many hours have passed while I engage in this habit.

While I'm not suggesting that you throw your televisions out, it's worth considering cutting back on viewing time. Statistics indicate that we dedicate approximately 1,825 hours per year to watching TV. Imagine the remarkable progress and accomplishments we could achieve if we allocated just one-third of this time toward pursuing our goals.

Most of us can honestly admit that we have developed some bad habits. Think about how you spend your time each day. Are you spending time in areas that won't help improve your tomorrows? If so, **decide to spend more time improving your mind, moving toward your goals, or building something of value – like yourself.**

People with purpose, drive, and goals often have distinct behaviors that set them apart from others. Most commonly, they do the following:

- Put more hours into work, goals, and dreams.
- Sleep less.
- Turn the TV off.
- Do what others will not.
- Read.
- Don't EVER stop learning.
- WORK AT BEING THEIR BEST!

While it's tempting to assume that time is abundant and everlasting, it passes by much more quickly than we realize. One day, you may ponder with introspection, questioning, "Where did the time go?" **Every single minute of your life matters.** To unlock your utmost potential, strive to **become a master of your time.**

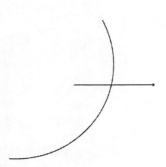

SET
Goals

7

Challenge Yourself to Set Goals that Inspire and Excite You.

"Setting goals is the first step in turning the invisible into the visible."

Tony Robbins

Goal setting has been ingrained in the teachings of countless business leaders and success coaches throughout history and for valid reasons. The concept itself is designed to compel you to envision a metaphorical carrot, a desirable outcome that inspires you to strive for greater achievements. By determining what your personal carrot represents, you can transform into an individual who possesses the necessary qualities and drive to attain it.

These quotes from Henry David Thoreau, Michelangelo, and Les Brown all emphasize the importance of setting goals and aiming high in life. Let's quickly break down the meaning behind each quote:

1. Henry David Thoreau: "In the long run, men hit only what they aim at." Thoreau suggests that **you can only achieve what you specifically aim for** and the significance of having a target or purpose in life.

2. Michelangelo: "The greatest danger for most of us is not that our aim is too high, and we miss it, but that it is too low, and we reach it." Michelangelo warns against setting low goals or settling for mediocrity. He believes **the real danger lies in not challenging yourself or not striving for your full potential.**

3. Les Brown: "Your goals are the road maps that guide you and show you what is possible for your life." Goals serve as road maps, providing direction and clarity on what is achievable and what path to take. **By setting goals, you create a vision of what you want to accomplish,** and they become the driving force that motivates and propels you forward.

Taken together, these quotes stress the importance of setting ambitious goals, aiming high, and continuously challenging yourself.

Numerous studies have shown that 83% of the population doesn't set goals. For those of us who are goal-setters, we find this hard to believe. I always assumed that everyone set goals like I had since I was a teen. But it's not the case. Though 14% of the population *thinks* about goals, they don't write them down, and only 3% of the population commits their goals to paper. Harvard Business School has done actual studies on this and found that the 14% of the population *with goals* are 10X more successful than the 83% who have none, and the 3% with *written* goals are 3X more successful than the 14%. I don't know about you, but those statistics alone motivate me to continue with my written goals.

As Yogi Berra, one of baseball's greats said, "If you don't know where you are going, you'll end up someplace else." Clear and articulate goals give you purpose, even if the road map isn't totally known. They also give you the motivation to work toward something important to you.

The act of **setting goals serves as a powerful catalyst for personal growth and transformation.** When you define a clear objective, you give shape and purpose to your ambitions. It then becomes a tangible manifestation of your aspirations, acting as a guiding light to steer you in the direction of success.

I personally write page after page of goals, and then I prioritize and categorize them when I'm done. If you're new to goal setting, start with this:

First, recall your vision for your life, then...

1. Write down either in a journal, on paper, or type on a computer as many goals as you can think of. Just brainstorm and see what you come up with. Don't worry about how well-defined they are, if they are practical, or even achievable. Just write everything that comes to mind.

Many experts will tell you to keep writing until you have written 100 goals.

2. Categorize your goals. Make headings for:
   a. Financial
   b. Business / Career
   c. Family / Relationships / Social
   d. Health / Fitness
   e. Self-Improvement

3. Prioritize all the brainstormed goals under each heading.

Congratulations, you've just committed your goals to paper. For me, this is always where I start. I have books dating back twenty years or more with my goals in them. I can easily review them and see what I've accomplished. I find I can cross many items off my lists as achieved, but then I also find that many goals no longer hold any importance. That's all fine as our lives change, as well as our circumstances and priorities. If I see an unachieved goal that seems to carry over year after year, I spend more time with it analyzing whether it's important to me. If so, I'll develop more ways to achieve it. If not, I'll let it slip away no longer holding importance.

Once your goals are committed to paper, some individuals expand upon them by turning them into SMART goals. Smart Goals help you to create a roadmap that empowers you to track your progress and adjust as you move forward. SMART goals are:

- Specific – Don't be vague. Write each goal very clearly and well-defined.
- Measurable – Quantify your goal.
- Attainable - Make sure the goal isn't so big you can't achieve it. But also, don't set it too low either.
- Realistic – Don't set a goal to be a professional basketball player if you're 5'2" and have never played before.
- Time Bound – Associate a deadline with each goal.

Though there are many programs, systems, and methods to establish, set, and write goals, I personally don't use any of them. I do what feels most comfortable for me – which are lists. For you, you may want to write a paragraph about each goal with great specificity. Maybe you want to dedicate a page to each goal with sub-goals. Maybe you want to use a computerized goal-setting program. No matter how you write your goals, I believe the simple act of committing them to paper will help you get closer to their realization. No matter where you write them down, however, **you must make it an active practice to review them daily and take some action toward them.** Goal setting isn't something you do on New Year's Day each year and then tuck away in a drawer and forget about it.

It's an ongoing activity. Note I used the word, *activity*, not process. It's something that needs to be worked into your daily routine.

For those goals of most importance, I do, however, go one step further. I write my goal on two post-It notes. I stick one on my bathroom mirror and one on my desk. These happen to be my two favorite areas. I like the bathroom mirror because I see it first thing in the morning and before I go to bed. It gets me thinking about my goals at the two most important times of the day. I also post a copy on my computer or desk, because for me, this is the place where I spend most of my time. For you, it may be on your refrigerator or even on your television. (It also may be a good deterrent to turn the tube off and go to work on your goal.) Keeping a goal in the forefront of your mind helps your subconscious to work on it – even when consciously, you aren't. Either way, it's a nice reminder.

And finally,

- Review your written goals daily.
- Add to them as new desires emerge.
- Jot down inspiration as to how to reach the goals.
- Focus on them several times a day.
- Take one action toward them daily.
- And don't forget to celebrate your successes by rewarding yourself when you reach one of your goals.

Whenever you decide to take a trip, you plan for it. You choose a date to leave, figure out how to get there, determine what hotels you want to stay at, what things you want to see, and when you will return home. Typically, every detail is carefully thought out. We do this for even the most mundane tasks and chores such as planning for dinner. You decide what you will make, go to the grocery store to get the ingredients needed, determine what time you want to eat, and begin making the necessary preparations. Preparing for events in your life is part of most individuals' normal processes. However, despite our proficiency in planning for and visualizing trips, preparing dinner, and handling everyday tasks, we frequently struggle when it comes to planning for significant things – such as our own lives!

The process of setting and pursuing goals fosters perseverance and demands dedication, focus, and self-accountability. By establishing clear targets, you hold yourself responsible for taking the necessary actions to achieve them. **Goals help to cultivate a proactive mindset and empower you to become the architect of your destiny.** It provides you with the tools and mindset needed to turn your dreams into reality. By envisioning and pursuing your *carrot*, you become the person capable of reaching it, transforming your aspirations into tangible achievements, and fulfilling your dreams.

"The thing that I learned early on is you need to set goals in your life, both short-term and long-term, just like you do in business. Having that long-term goal will enable you to have a plan on how to achieve it." Denise Morrison

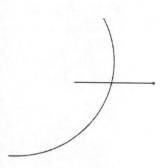

SURROUND YOURSELF
WITH THE RIGHT

Your Tribe are Those Who Help You Reach Higher and Achieve More.

"You will rarely make wise decisions if you surround yourself with fools."

Rasheed Ogunlaru

There are two main types of resources: capital and people. If you want to succeed, achieve your goals, and live the life you desire, you'll want to surround yourself with the right people.

Statistics show us that we are the average of the five people we spend the most time with. Who do you spend your time with? Are you surrounding yourself with individuals who show no inclination to improve their lives? Those who lack direction in both their personal and professional endeavors? Those who complain incessantly but don't take any action to change the situation? While it's important to avoid passing judgment on these people, it's equally important to distance yourself from those who don't positively contribute to your life. Without realizing it, their presence can decrease your motivation and ambition and pull you down into their mindset and behaviors.

Being mindful of the company you keep is vital for your mindset and personal growth, as it directly impacts your ability to become the best version of yourself. It is essential to actively seek out people who are positive and uplifting. **And it is more important to surround yourself with those who encourage your successes, support your goals and ambitions, and bring out the best in you.** Rationally, this all makes sense as you want to be around people who make you feel good. However, it's not always so clear-cut.

As our business grew, we had to hire more employees to help with clients' workloads. Externally, one of these individuals was competent in her job but an extremely negative person. Like cancer, her negative statements, constant complaints, and doom-and-gloom personality began to slowly grow and infect others. It wasn't long before other team members began to mimic her negativity, while others were brought down by her presence creating an environment in the workplace that was no longer enjoyable or uplifting. It's important to understand how much of an influence one bad apple can have on those around it.

Many people like to be the smartest, prettiest, or most successful person in the business and social groups they belong to. But if you do this, you ultimately hurt yourself. If you're the best in the group, how will you grow? Who will push you to be better? Yes, you may be able to help those around you improve, but how do they help you to improve?

Every successful person knows the importance of others in achieving their goals and dreams. It's not a one-man (or woman) job unless you're a hermit or living in a remote cave with no interaction with others. Achieving a truly successful life requires a diverse group of individuals with unique talents that complement your own. Recognizing this, you come to **understand the significance of surrounding yourself with exceptional people.** Often, these are the people who surpass you in various aspects and excel in areas where you may struggle. They serve as a source of inspiration and facilitate your personal growth. It's these people who can play a pivotal role in helping you realize your dreams and unlock your fullest potential.

John C. Maxwell states, "If you have great people around you, they will take you higher than your dream will. Leaders are never self-made. Those closest to you determine your level of success, so choosing the right companions as partners in pursuit of your vision is an important decision. My advice is to surround yourself with talented people who will challenge you, help you grow, and inspire you to maximize your potential." We need good partners, mentors, and friends.

Think about the five people you spend the most time with, but in doing so, it's important to approach this assignment without personal judgment and only look at it as a strategic exercise.

Consider the level of positivity and support these five people bring to your life. Do they uplift and encourage you, or do they tend to be negative and unsupportive? Assess their values and goals. Do they align with your values? Are they motivated to succeed? Are they open to self-improvement? Do they seek new opportunities and challenges? What overall impact do they have on your mental and emotional well-being?

Think about these factors and begin by assigning a rating based on their positive influence on your life. Remember this exercise is meant to help you reflect on the dynamics of your relationships and not pass judgment. Assign each person a rating from one to ten.

A "ten" would be someone who:
- Is inspiring.
- Is motivating.
- Is supportive.
- Makes you want to be better.
- Elevates your thinking.
- Fuels your energy.
- Makes you think outside of the box.
- Makes you feel good to be around.
- Talks about things of value, not people.
- Encourages new ideas and decisions.

A "one" would be someone who:

- Brings others down.
- Is a naysayer.
- Focuses on what is wrong.
- Says things that make you question yourself or your decisions.
- Drains your energy.
- Talks about others.
- Always has a crisis or problem.
- Talks about themselves or overtalks others.

These are but a few examples, but I'm certain you understand the concept. After you've done this for your five people, determine their average score. *(Add all five scores and divide that number by five to get your average score.)* Are you happy with the number you calculated? Would you like to increase it? Then rate yourself. How do you fall within this range? Most often you will find, if you're honest, **you are the exact average of your group.**

If you find this of value, then maybe do this for the top ten people you spend the most time with. It will help you to determine if there is someone in your group who is bringing your average down and if it's time to rethink who you surround yourself with. With the right people around you, all things are possible. With the wrong people, you'll most likely be stuck where you are with little growth possibilities.

The company you keep has a profound impact on your life. The individuals you choose to surround yourself with can either lift you up or hold you back. So, when I say, surround yourself with people better than yourself, I'm not trying to imply a sense of inferiority or inadequacy. Rather, I'm speaking to your desired growth and self-improvement. Being in the presence of those who are better than us challenges us to rise to their level or above. It motivates us to push beyond our comfort zones and strive for excellence. It fosters an environment of inspiration, and most of all, it broadens our perspectives and exposes us to new ideas.

Seeing others excel and achieve pushes you to overcome self-imposed limitations and tap into your untapped potential. It propels you toward setting higher standards and surpassing your previous achievements. The positive energy and collective ambition of those striving for greatness can fuel your own motivation and inspire you to consistently raise the bar. This often becomes a catalyst for personal growth and empowers you to unlock your full potential. So, in your pursuit of growth, be mindful of the people you have in your inner circle.

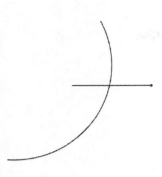

NETWORK AND BUILD
Relationships

A Successful Life is Never Achieved Alone.

"Your network is your net worth."

Porter Gale

Being young and untested in my industry, I quickly learned **the significance of networking and building relationships.** This invaluable skill set was one that I began to cultivate, hone, and develop in my formative years of business, and I can attest to the profound impact it has had on my personal and professional growth.

I have a vivid memory of attending a speaking event given by Brian Tracy, recognized as one of the most influential motivational speakers of our time. During this talk, Tracy stressed the importance of networking, highlighting its potential to act as a gateway to a multitude of opportunities. He underscored that every interaction holds the potential to forge a lasting connection that may prove fruitful in the future. Connecting with others may also often open doors that would otherwise remain closed.

Tracy's words resonated deeply with me, and upon arriving home after this event, I purchased a Rolodex. (For those of you who may be too young to know what a Rolodex is, it was a rotating card file device where you could store business contact information.) Armed with my Rolodex, I embarked on a personal quest to actively build and expand my network. Any time I engaged in conversations with acquaintances and professionals in various industries, I sought to meet new people and foster connections. The Rolodex became a tangible manifestation of my commitment to networking, serving as a reminder of the importance of cultivating relationships.

Today, the digital age has rendered my physical Rolodex obsolete, yet its essence and purpose continue to thrive in the virtual realm. Through this realm, we can build our network and nurture our connections at a far greater speed and a much further reach. Regardless, the principles behind networking go unchanged: the cultivation of genuine relationships, the willingness to extend support, and the openness to seize opportunities presented by every interaction.

The importance of networking and building relationships resonated so deeply within me that I made it a priority to instill this value in my son from an early age. I felt interacting with a wide range of individuals cultivated his ability to communicate effectively and expand his view of life. Fueled by his passion for baseball, from the age of ten he reached out to professional players, coaches, and team owners. To my astonishment, several of these individuals reached back. By the age of thirteen, he had cultivated a network of relationships in the baseball trading card industry, earning him a reputation as one of the foremost experts in his field. As the years progressed, his dedication to building relationships grew and transcended into his business success. He ultimately began doing business with the world's top athletes and some of the most recognizable names in business today.

Witnessing the impact networking and relationship building had on my son's journey affirmed the importance I placed on these skills. It reinforced the belief that genuine connections, nurtured with sincerity and authenticity, can pave the way for remarkable opportunities and accomplishments.

View networking as an essential component in achieving your goals while keeping in mind that it is also a two-way street. It's not just about reaping benefits from your connections, but also about being there for them. Networking is often viewed as a method to achieve your goals or advance your own interests. While this perspective isn't entirely incorrect, it fails to acknowledge the true essence of networking – understanding the essential component in achieving not only your goals but also in helping others achieve theirs.

In a world that thrives on connections and relationships, networks serve as a conduit for opportunities, knowledge, and support. It's a web of interconnections that allows us to expand our horizons, explore new possibilities, and reach new heights. However, it should never be reduced to a self-serving endeavor. Instead, it should be approached with a genuine willingness to offer assistance and support to others. It's a give-and-take relationship where you can share expertise, resources, and insight. It can foster growth, collaboration, and success. Strengthening the bonds of our network creates a sense of fulfillment and purpose and reinforces our commitment to continue to build meaningful relationships.

My encounter with Brian Tracy provided me with a tangible tool, and then witnessing my son's use of this tool proved as a testament to the transformative power of networking and building relationships. The skills and connections established laid the groundwork for personal and professional growth. When you embrace the mindset of networking, it ultimately paves the way for success and fulfillment. I urge you to welcome the power of connections, seek out relationships, and invest in building lasting bonds, knowing that these efforts will reap rewards that extend far into the future.

To begin your journey into networking, here are a few steps you can take.

1. **Determine why you want to network.** Are you looking for job opportunities, seeking mentors, or trying to expand your personal or professional connections?

2. **Determine who you want to connect with.** Consider professionals in your field, industry experts, colleagues, and individuals from organizations or clubs you're interested in. This will help you to tailor your networking approach.

3. **Reach out to people you already know,** such as friends, family members, or former colleagues. They may be able to introduce you to individuals who can help you with your networking goals.

4. **Look for professional events,** conferences, seminars, or events in the field you have an interest in. These gatherings provide excellent opportunities to meet like-minded people.

5. **Join professional organizations or clubs** of personal interest. Attend their meetings and events.

6. **Use social media and platforms like LinkedIn** to build and expand your network.

7. **Engage in conversations, exchange contact information, and follow up and maintain relationships.**

Advancement, success, and all achievements in life typically stem from personal relationships. Developing these relationships is key. But also keep in mind that networking and building relationships is an ongoing process. Be patient, persistent, and genuine in your efforts. Over time, you will develop and build a strong network that can bring mutual benefits to both your life and those of your network.

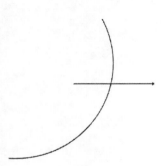

10

BE FINANCIALLY
Responsible

Your Wealth Mindset is More Important Than Your Income.

"The philosophy of the rich and the poor is this: the rich invest their money and spend what is left. The poor spend their money and invest what is left."

Robert Kiyosaki

By my early thirties, my husband and I owned several companies in the financial sector, we had just started a venture capital firm, and I saw a wide variety of clients. All of this gave me an incredible opportunity to witness how a vast array of people handled their financial affairs. Also, it forced me to become extremely knowledgeable in a wide range of low-risk investments to unconventional high-risk ones depending on my client's needs and wants. And most of all, I learned how to best handle the financial affairs of our companies for their greatest growth and prosperity.

Whether for my clients or the businesses we ran, finances and investments were always at the forefront of my thinking. I loved to delve into the mindset of successful business owners and my wealthier clients to try to figure out what worked in building wealth and what didn't. I had clients in their twenties, eighties, and everywhere in between. Some were just starting out trying to gain a bit of financial independence, while others were multi-millionaires. Some were lottery winners, professional athletes, and international celebrities, while others were teachers, small business owners, and farmers. It didn't matter what their profession or status was. All had similar commonalities based on their financial mindset.

First, there were the lottery winners. They came into a great deal of money, yet they all tended to be cash rich and wealth-mindset-poor. No matter the advice and guidance given, they chose not to follow it, save, or invest. Having money meant the opportunity to spend whatever they wanted, and this was what they did. It didn't matter how many millions they had won, they soon found themselves over-extended and in financial difficulty within a few years. According to Credit Donkey, 70% of lottery winners file for bankruptcy or go broke. Though these people had the opportunity for great wealth, they spent it frivolously and ended up back where they began. They didn't have a wealth mindset, or the fortitude to protect the money they had won.

I also found this mentality prevailed in the professional services field. Many clients who were doctors, for example, made great incomes but tended to spend it all on big houses, the latest and greatest toys such as boats and other recreational vehicles, and extravagant vacations. They were often more concerned with appearances than with protecting their wealth. When it came time to invest for their future or retirement, they often came up short.

You can have all the money in the world or make a great income, but if it slips through your fingers by spending it trying to keep up appearances of wealth, you will never be wealthy.

Then there were the teachers. These people were my steady Eddies. Each week, they invested a portion of their paycheck into their tax-sheltered annuity retirement plan. They were conservative in their spending and more active in their savings. By the time they retired, they had accumulated great sums of retirement funds. They were forward thinkers and preparers for their future, but they also were a bit conservative in their investment strategy. They understood the importance of compounding wealth and dollar-cost averaging, and as a result, most achieved their financial goals. But they were also at times too conservative, which often kept them from true wealth.

Finally, there were the clients whom I considered to have a wealth mindset. They seemed to have an approach to wealth that separated them from everyone else. They were like my teachers in that they spent conservatively and made regular investments, but they also were always looking for ways to improve their financial standing. They weren't excessive risk-takers, but their habits, beliefs, and behaviors seem to separate them from the rest. They invested their money in themselves, in their knowledge, in their businesses, and in areas of potential growth or areas that produced multiple streams of income. Then, and only then, did they spend what was left. Most people spend first and only invest IF there is anything left.

I also learned that wealth goes beyond just the amount of income one earns. It's not solely about the money coming in; rather, it's about the growth and accumulation of assets over time. Focusing on the growth of assets, rather than fixating solely on income, is a characteristic of individuals with a wealth mindset.

When evaluating your wealth, it's important to look at the bigger picture of financial well-being. While a high income can provide immediate financial comfort, it doesn't guarantee long-term wealth if assets aren't growing. **By shifting the focus from income to asset growth, individuals can adopt a more sustainable and strategic approach to a wealth mindset.**

To further explain this concept, someone earning $250,000 a year might seem financially successful and secure, but if their assets remain stagnant or decline, they aren't necessarily building long-term wealth. On the other hand, an individual earning $50,000 a year and having assets that are growing through smart investments and savings are increasing their wealth for the long term.

A good way to track this is to keep a spreadsheet listing all your assets and valuing them. List items such as savings accounts, checking accounts, money markets, stock trading accounts, retirement plans, real estate, physical assets like gold and silver, loan receivables, and all other assets you might have. Then list everything you owe on those assets, (such as mortgages, car loans, student debt, credit card debts, etc.) and deduct the total of this amount from your asset total. This is your true net worth. You might review these numbers every six months to see if you are on track for building your wealth or not. It's a way to look at the bigger picture than only looking at your income, as income can change or stop at any point.

Total Assets – Minus Debt and Payables = Net Worth

While cultivating a wealth mindset is a significant step toward financial responsibility, it's important to acknowledge that it can be challenging for many individuals. You may find yourself in a situation where making ends meet is a constant struggle. Trust me, I've been there too. There was a time in my life when my meals consisted of boxes of macaroni and cheese and Ramon noodles. I also lived in an apartment where my furniture was limited to a bed, a desk, and a chair. And you know what? I was okay with that. I had a place to sleep and a place to work. It was all I needed. During that time, I didn't focus on what I didn't have. I focused on where I wanted to go and how to get there.

Just as we spoke earlier in Chapter 6 about managing your time and the hours in a day, this same concept can be applied to your financial situation.

There are typically always expenses that can be cut to help reduce your monthly expense burden. Many will immediately respond to this statement and insist there are no expenses that can be reduced. You may question it as well, but if you honestly look at where your money is going, there are always areas.

Most people are unable to accurately account for their weekly expenses, let alone their monthly. They forget that they bought a latte at Starbucks, got take-out for lunch, or stopped at Target on the way home to pick up a few things – and we all know what happens when we do that! We go in for one item and come out with five or more. Most don't review their phone and cable bills to see if there are channels they could cut out, or if other phone plans could be more cost-effective.

It's all about paying attention to expenses both personally and in your business. During the "less than adequate financial period of my life," I didn't have a television, which saved me the expense of cable. I used the time I may have spent watching Netflix to work on myself and my business instead. It saved me a lot more than the $150 per month it may have cost me. It helped me focus on what was important by not being distracted! **Being more aware helps make you more responsible.**

It's important to remember that in your life, two things truly hold significant value: your health and your time. These are two areas that are worth far more than material wealth and what it can buy. While some may choose to invest in extravagant possessions like a fancy car to impress others, the thrill is often short-lived as newer and better versions emerge. Possessions only provide temporary happiness. After you drive the car for a while, you realize that regardless of the make or model, it's still a piece of metal that gets you from one place to another. In the grand scheme of life, it holds little importance.

Possessions alone cannot help you achieve your financial goals or attain financial independence. As Epictetus wisely said, **"Wealth consists not in having great possessions, but in having few wants."** This is a key to financial success. It's not the accumulation of things that defines your worth or brings lasting fulfillment. The fewer desires you have, the more rapidly you can accumulate money to invest in yourself, investments, and business ventures. By reducing your wants and cultivating the mindset of simplicity, you create opportunities to allocate your resources toward endeavors that truly enrich your life and bring you genuine prosperity.

Yet, in my opinion, being financially responsible is not just in your ability to keep expenses in check, earn a living, or in building your assets. It's in your ability to realize that YOU control your money, wealth, and financial situation. Ayn Rand stated, *"Money is only a tool. It will take you wherever you wish, but it will not replace you as the driver."*

Ask yourself these questions to help you to understand what your money mindset may currently be.

- What were you taught as a child about money?

- What do you currently believe about money?

- What are your current beliefs about rich people? Poor people?

- How do you see yourself? Rich? Poor? Average?

- What are you currently spending your money on, and why?

- If you had more money, what would you do with it?

- Why do you want more money?

Your beliefs and thoughts about money play a crucial role in shaping your financial outcomes. If you consistently dwell on scarcity and lack, you're more likely to attract more of the same. Likewise, if you prioritize spending over saving and investing, you'll find yourself constantly chasing after new things to buy and depleting your financial resources.

It's important to recognize that your mindset regarding wealth and prosperity can have a profound impact on your financial situation. If you hold the belief that only the rich get richer, you inadvertently place yourself in the category of those who do not possess wealth, rather than aligning yourself with those who do.

To alter your financial trajectory, it's necessary to shift your mindset and beliefs about money. Cultivate an abundance mentality, focusing on the possibilities and opportunities available to you. Instead of dwelling on lack, direct your thoughts toward abundance, prosperity, and financial success. Develop thankfulness for all you have and be truly grateful for all the abundance already in your life. This change in perspective can open doors to new avenues of wealth creation and financial growth.

Embracing the value of saving and investing is another essential step toward achieving financial well-being. Be grateful for what you earn or have saved. Focus on the positive things that money can do for you instead of looking for ways to spend it. And focus on positive beliefs and thoughts regarding money. A simple affirmation you may use is one that the book, *The Secret*, taught us. **"Money comes easily and frequently to me in small and large amounts."** With good financial habits and patience, you will soon generate a foundation for future financial stability. By adopting a mindset of abundance, valuing saving and investing, and rejecting limiting beliefs, you can shift the trajectory of your financial journey toward prosperity and success.

"Both abundance and lack exist simultaneously in our lives, as parallel realities. It is always our conscious choice which secret garden we will tend. When we choose to be grateful for the abundance that's present — love, health, family, friends, work, the joys of nature, and personal pursuits that bring us pleasure — the wasteland of lack falls away and we experience heaven on Earth." Sarah Ban Breathnach

11

LIFE ISN'T ALWAYS
Fair

Life Satisfaction is Always Based on Your Perception.

"If life is unfair with everyone,
doesn't that make life fair?"

Thabang Gideon Magaola

Life isn't always fair. Accepting this reality is essential. It can be challenging when you genuinely believe that your efforts should entitle you to more than what you have received. It's natural to feel a sense of injustice as you observe others seemingly receiving more than their fair share. You may feel emotions of frustration, resentment, or even anger. Sometimes, life isn't fair, but it's important not to let these feelings become an excuse for inaction. It's not about what you think you deserve, but rather about the actions you take to shape your future.

My best advice is **don't compare and don't focus on others.** The more you focus on others, the less you focus on yourself, who you want to be, and where you want to go. The more you focus on others, the more you hold yourself back in a perceived state of lack. Don't compare. Everyone is on a different journey, and sometimes these people will have challenges that you may not wish on your worst enemy. So don't worry about what they are doing or compare their lives to yours. Just focus on what you are doing and your own personal development.

"Greatness is best measured by how well an individual responds to the happenings in life that appear to be totally unfair, unreasonable, and undeserved." – Marvin J. Ashton

In life, there will always be people who earn more money than you do, are in seemingly better relationships, and maybe are even better-looking than you. However, it's equally important to acknowledge that there are also those people who have a lot less in all these areas compared to you. **While life may appear unfair, upon introspection, you might discover that it is also unfair in *your favor* at times as well.**

In the grand scheme of things, the world maintains a delicate balance. You find yourself positioned in the middle of the teeter-totter, surrounded by people on both ends. On one side some are thrust up into the air on the teeter-totter, flying high in life, and experiencing success, exhilaration, and triumph. On the other end, however, are those sitting on the ground facing their own challenges. Life should not be approached as a competition where all strive to be elevated on the teeter-totter at the same time. We all have different backgrounds, talents, and challenges. We don't all have to be in the same place at the same time. Don't spend your energy on comparisons.

This brings me to a story about one of my assistants. When my business grew to a point where I couldn't help everyone personally, I brought on an assistant. I taught her everything about the business, gave her my smaller clients, and took her to all my speaking events to teach her about networking. Even though I was her mentor, I considered her a friend and did everything I could to help further her position with the company and in life.

However, she didn't feel the same. Although to my face, she acted as though I was the best thing since sliced bread, behind my back she said unflattering things. When she was confronted with the question of why, she attributed it to a sense of envy. She believed that I had been granted "everything," while she had been left with mere "scraps." Her jealousy and the perception that she deserved more stemmed from a detrimental habit of comparing her life to others – an approach that seldom leads to success. In her eyes, life seemed unfair because she believed I possessed more than her.

When you achieve a level of success that appears to be "better" than another's, you have a good chance of becoming a **target of resentment.** You can also become a target simply for being better looking than another, having a better relationship, or appearing to be more popular. It's not uncommon for someone to find aspects about you that they may resent. In such instances, there is a good chance of becoming a target of animosity, driven by the subjective interpretation of what is fair.

Being a CEO or holding a position of authority is undeniably challenging. In any such role, there will always be individuals who resent you and perceive it as *unfair* for whatever reason. Throughout my journey, I've witnessed people in these positions being taken advantage of, targeted, and resented. Whether these acts and perceptions were fair or not remains open to interpretation. Thinking may have been clouded on the individual's part or the CEO's. However, in the grand scheme of things everything tends to balance out. So, when you look at your life and think you got the short end of the stick, shortchanged, or are at a disadvantage, consider this: What you perceive are only the leaves on the tree. What you fail to see are the roots that endured darkness and dampness to foster the growth of the trunk, and eventually those leaves. Your perspective captures only a fleeting moment in time. **No matter how convinced you are that someone else has a "better" or "more" fulfilling life, know there is always more to the story.**

Instead of dwelling on comparisons and assumptions, focus on nurturing your own growth and embracing your own journey. Appreciate the roots that have shaped your path and remember that everyone's roots are different. Each person's story is complex and layered and often conceals hidden struggles and sacrifices. So, when you start having feelings of entitlement due to your belief that life should be fair:

1. Acknowledge that you are feeling this way. Ask yourself, why don't I think this is fair?

2. Analyze whether these feelings are logical thoughts or emotional thoughts. Sometimes, when we start to think about a situation logically, we realize there is no basis for these feelings. Example: When my assistant with two years of experience in business compared herself to me with almost twenty, there should have been no comparison. Realize that you may be on Chapter 2 when the other person is on Chapter 20.

3. Look beyond yourself. When you start having feelings of resentment, comparison, or an unfair life, try to look at it beyond your personal situation. Try to see the person or situation through their eyes.

4. Try to change your perception. Maybe you can do this by getting to know the person better. However, you will never fully know another without walking in their shoes for a lifetime. You don't know how many demons they had to fight to get where they are. No one's life is perfect – no matter how it appears to be. If you look close enough, you can always find something that balances the scales.

5. Let it go and focus on your own life!

Have compassion for everyone, don't compare, and don't focus on others. **Life isn't always fair, but somehow, in the end, it just may be!**

12

CONQUER YOUR *Fears*

On the Other Side of Fear are Endless Possibilities.

"Thinking will not overcome fear, but action will."

W. Clement Stone

Fear can easily hold you back in life. It may be a fear of failure. It could be a fear of making a change. It could even be a fear of what others might think about you. When fear sets in, it becomes a paralyzing state where you may feel you can't move forward. Standing still, however, is a true failure because it limits you.

"The fears we don't face become our limits." – Robin Sharma

As our companies grew, we eventually merged them into a public company. Several years later we found ourselves unexpectedly entangled in a merger that developed into a hostile takeover battle. The company trying to gain control clandestinely initiated efforts to drive the price of our stock down. Of course, we tried to protect our shareholders, but the negative publicity the company received cast doubt and skepticism among shareholders, which led to many of them hastily selling off their shares. As the stock dropped, we suffered the loss of shareholders, clients, and even friendships during this challenging period. Shortly after, the rival company seized the opportunity and acquired the majority stake in the company.

This experience shattered me as I witnessed how quickly our company became a target. It was devastating to see people's loyalty and support dissipate in an instant. It was also disheartening to realize that those who once held us in high regard suddenly jumped on the bandwagon of blame and dislike when they felt there was nothing more for them to gain from our association. As someone who wholeheartedly devoted myself to helping others, this sudden turn of events left me devastated and feeling greatly betrayed.

The impact of this ordeal on my perception of people was profound. It left an indelible mark that eroded my faith in others. The sense of betrayal and pain ran so deep that I found myself no longer wanting to help others or have anything to do with anyone outside of my family and a small circle of loyal friends. The wounds inflicted by this experience also created a sense of fear of something like this happening again, and it became a barrier that prevented me from any enjoyment of a career that I once loved. So, eventually, I left the company, sold my book of business, and retired. "There!" I said to myself, "I will never have to deal with people ever again!" But life doesn't work that way.

Looking back, while it wasn't a pleasant experience to go through, I was proud of what we had accomplished. We created a lot of careers, supported several growing companies, provided clients with conservative asset management, and never missed an interest or dividend payment on our stock or bonds.

The irony of the situation was that a few years later we joined forces with the majority shareholders to once again fight off yet another hostile takeover from another company. This turned out to be the right decision as several years later the company was acquired by a New York investment bank for fifty-five million dollars, and three years later, the company was re-acquired again for one hundred million dollars. The company that was started with a $3,400 credit card loan and the public company that was once selling for $.10 a share, was now acquired for close to $10.00 a share. Those shareholders that had stuck with us were finally rewarded for their loyalty and support.

The fear of being hurt is a natural response to protect ourselves from potential pain and disappointment. It's a self-preservation mechanism that arises from the desire to avoid future harm. However, it's important to recognize that allowing fear to dominate our lives can limit our growth and prevent us from realizing our full potential. I knew I had to eventually overcome my fear of dishonest people and what I thought was betrayal by others, or I would never be able to move forward and build positive connections again. It took time, and I still carry a bit of caution from this experience inside, but it no longer controls me.

At some point in life, we all encounter experiences that instill fear-based thoughts. It could be a traumatic event, a past failure, or even specific phobias like the fear of public speaking or the fear of change that may ignite it. I recall following a severe car accident that left my vehicle completely wrecked and with the police expressing surprise at my survival. As a result, for quite some time after, I developed an excessive level of caution and fear of having another accident when it came to driving. If you ask my friends now, however, they will tell you that I have completely overcome that fear!

Can you think of a time when you developed a fear-based thought? Do you know any women who may want a divorce but are afraid to pursue it for fear of how their lifestyle might change and what others may think? Do you know a woman who would like to leave her current employment but fears her inability to start over? Maybe you know of someone who is extremely shy and won't express her opinion due to her fear of being laughed at or rejected. This list could go on forever as there are an insurmountable number of fears we can conjure up in life. But the point is, we can internalize a lot of outside events and turn them into some sort of internalized fear-based limitation if we let it.

It's not until we overcome our fears that we will truly be free from them.

Keep in mind when we speak of fear, we are not talking about true danger and fear that comes because of our innate survival mechanism. This type of fear keeps us alert and ready to handle any unforeseen situation. We are talking about "imagined" threats – threats we have created, *or accepted* in our mind due to trauma, experiences, phobias, or perceived adverse situations. This type of fear comes in many forms. If you are being brutally beaten by your husband, however, this is a true threat and justifiable fear. When you are afraid to leave your house because you believe you will be run over by a speeding car, this is most likely an *imagined* fear holding you back. Covid, however, became an example of a hybrid of fears. Covid was a real and imagined threat and became a fear of such great proportion that it changed the world, how we interact with others, and how we work.

Being scared at times is perfectly acceptable, but you can't let it determine your fate. If you do, it will hold you back from opportunities, your ultimate potential, and your happiness 100% of the time. You will need to get to a point where you decide you are not going to let fear win or take control of your life. When you are faced with an "imagined" version of fear, Zig Ziglar says you have two options: Forget Everything and Run, or Face Everything and Rise.

Overcoming fear requires acknowledging and understanding what contributed to the fear. I didn't realize for quite some time that my true fear was of being hurt again by people I trusted and cared for – my clients, my so-called friends, and my business associates. I felt betrayed by them all. I didn't want to give anyone a chance to betray me again. Once I realized what the root of my fear was, I placed my focus on what I desired and not what I feared. I began to take small steps in letting people into my life once again. Yes, I was cautious about who I let in. Trust me, the vetting process was brutal! But the more steps I took, I soon found myself back on the horse making new friends and building a new business.

Taking small steps outside of your comfort zone helps to conquer fears. This may entail seeking support from trusted friends, seeking professional guidance, or engaging in gradual exposure to the source of your fear. By slowly facing and navigating through these challenges, you can build resilience and confidence, proving to yourself that you have the strength to overcome whatever your fear may be. Dale Carnegie stated, "Do the thing you fear to do and keep on doing it. That is the quickest and surest way ever yet discovered to conquer fear."

You may still find yourself afraid. You may still feel fear surrounding whatever it is that is holding you back, but the more you face it, eventually its grip on you will lessen. And one day you will make a choice that fear will *not* determine the course of your life! **The life you envisioned for yourself is still there. It's just on the other side of fear.** So, it's okay to be afraid, but don't let it stop you. Go after the life that is still waiting for you.

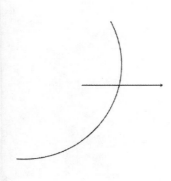

CHANGE AND
Grow

You Can't Grow Unless You are Willing to Change.

"If we don't change, we don't grow. If we don't grow, we aren't really living."

Gail Sheehy

You've probably heard the saying, "If you aren't growing, you're dying." I believe this encapsulates the essence of life. Continuous growth seems to nourish our souls and bring fulfillment. However, when people discuss *growth*, they often confuse it with the concept of *change*. While there are similarities between the two, there exists a significant distinction. **Change typically originates from outside or external sources and is visible in its manifestation.** For example, a move to a new home represents a noticeable change. Whereas **growth seems to emanate from within, from our internal processes.** It's often intangible and not immediately visible to others.

In the journey of life, we encounter numerous changes. We transition from the comfort of our parents' home to attend college, and most likely enter a few different relationships along the way. Eventually, some of us get married and have children, and some experience the complexity of divorce and remarriage. According to statistics, it's not uncommon for a person to live in as many as eleven different places in their lifetime. And, according to the Bureau of Labor Statistics, an average person will have twelve jobs and change careers five to seven times.

I have lived in eleven different homes, in two states, have been divorced, and have made several changes to my career over my lifetime. **External changes are easy to quantify and see and contribute to the rich tapestry of our experiences.** Yet, while changes may feel unsettling or uncertain, it's often through these transitions that we uncover hidden strengths, embrace new passions, and embark on transformative journeys.

Growth is much harder to measure.

Throughout the course of my life, as I navigated through these various milestones and experiences, one constant remained: an abundance of lessons to be learned and the undeniable necessity for change and growth. While the external changes in my life were readily apparent, it was the internal growth that proved to be indispensable and carried me through numerous challenges and experiences. I'm certain you can list several times that you have experienced a change in your life. Change may also be the answer to achieving some of your goals.

Change is inevitable. But why is it so different than growth?

- Change can be made in an instant. Growth takes time.

- Change can be negative or positive. Growth is typically always positive.
- Change can be (but doesn't necessarily have to be) the beginning of growth.
- Growth always begins with a desire for change.
- Change can be forced. Growth is self-motivated.
- Change can be short-lived. Growth is everlasting.

John Maxwell said, "Change is inevitable. Growth is optional." There could be no truer statement. Our journeys in life will allow us to have numerous experiences, meet various people, make mistakes, and succeed. The key lies in our interpretation of these changes and the lessons we glean from them. Change can be intimidating for many, and it is understandable, as certain changes can be disruptive and cause pain and heartache. Not all changes are pleasant. However, upon reflection, can you look back and identify moments in your life when even the most challenging changes yielded something positive? That a lesson was learned? That it contributed to some internal growth?

Change, despite its difficulties, often acts as a catalyst for personal transformation. It presents us with opportunities to adapt, learn, and develop resilience. Though it may be uncomfortable and require us to step outside our comfort zones, change has the potential to shape us and spark internal growth.

Before change or growth can take place, however, typically these components exist:

1) There is an **awareness** that changes, or growth needs to take place. Being conscious and clear about a situation is always the first step to taking steps toward moving forward.

2) There is a **desire** for change or growth. If the desire doesn't exist, change or growth won't happen. There must be desire. Yet, awareness and desire aren't enough.

3) Wishing for change or growth doesn't make it happen. You must **commit to what, why, and how** – **What** you want to change. **Why** it's so important to change, and **how** you intend to achieve it. Commitment to change is a necessary component.

4) And finally, **action** is what ultimately makes change and growth possible.

As change takes place in your life, you may find:

Change can make you braver. By facing changes head-on and believing them to be positive, it helps you to face challenges in a similar manner.

Consider every change a positive opportunity. It's all about shifting your perspective.

Change can help you to become flexible. Those who are the most flexible tend to adapt more quickly. They are seen as stable and reliable and are valued for their calm demeanor toward change. As a result, they are seen as being more positive individuals.

Change can help you to be grateful. When change occurs, it may help you to recognize areas that you may have taken for granted. It allows you to compare one situation to another, although it's important you don't judge them. Accept and be grateful.

Change can help you to succeed. Every moment of change brings potential opportunities. Though change isn't always easy, if you embrace it and make it work for you, you will attract more positive opportunities in the long run.

However, as with all aspects of life, once you feel like you've reached a point where you believe you have fulfilled your goals and desires, change will often tug at you and urge you to continue to grow. I was retired and enjoying family, writing, and friends. But then I was faced with a divorce. It was yet another time in my life that would require change and inner growth. It was also a time of great contemplation to figure out what I wanted the next chapter of my life to hold. I focused on the positive, looked at it as an opportunity, and began a consulting business.

Soon I attracted a national franchise that became a full-time consulting job of monitoring all their financial aspects, overseeing their audits, ghost-writing books for them, and training their employees. It was a great opportunity as it provided an excellent income, and I was able to schedule my work whenever I wanted, which allowed me to still play tennis with friends in the mornings. But then, three years later, the change-mobile arrived. I was told they wanted to move everything I did in-house and offered me a full-time position. While it would have most likely been a decent opportunity, it would mean a 9-5 job, five days a week, and my working for someone else versus for myself – meaning I no longer had control over my work schedule. I ultimately turned it down and agreed to train someone who wanted the position. Yet by doing this, I was now faced with trying to figure out what else I'd do with my time. I decided that continuing to grow my consulting business would be the best move.

I went to FedEx to print new business cards. While there, I met a gentleman who asked what I did. Long story, short, this was my introduction to the solar business. After several conversations, I agreed to come on and run a start-up for a small ownership position. I knew nothing about the solar industry but figured I could run any company. I just had to learn the product.

All these changes could have been daunting and scary for me. But I didn't let myself wallow in a state of fear. I stayed flexible to the opportunities that presented themselves. Once an opportunity came about, I knew it was there for a reason, and I was grateful. Then with commitment and determination, as well as newfound internal growth, I pressed forward to succeed. The key for me was to not focus on what was lost or the situation before the change. It was to develop excitement for the new opportunity, stay positive, and be grateful for what was in store. The tougher part was not the external change, but the inner growth it would take to step into the next chapter of my life.

As I mentioned earlier, change is a constant presence in our lives, and often it is the most uncomfortable situations that provide us with the greatest growth opportunities. In the words of Leon Brown, **"Life does not always give you what you want, but if you look closely, you will see that it gives you what you need for your growth."**

Consider what might be preventing you from experiencing growth. Is there something you aspire to achieve in life but find yourself holding back? Are you afraid of making changes? Don't let fear or your insecurities hinder your progress. Embracing change can lead to incredible opportunities that you may never have experienced without taking risks. Don't be afraid of change; instead, let it guide you toward personal growth.

Recognize that growth often occurs outside of our comfort zones. It requires courage, resilience, and a willingness to step into the unknown. By letting go of fear and embracing change, you open yourself up to a world of opportunities and transformative experiences. Embrace change because this is where you will discover growth and your true capabilities.

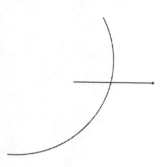

SEIZE OPPORTUNITIES
AND TAKE A
Chance

Become a Magnet that Attracts Opportunities to You.

"Your regrets aren't what you did, but what you didn't do. So, I take every opportunity."

Cameron Diaz

I'm a true believer in seizing opportunities and in taking chances. I feel that if an opportunity finds its way onto my path, there's a reason for it. If it feels good, I pursue it. As I mentioned previously, I was literally at FedEx having business cards printed to market myself as a consultant when I met someone who said he might have a potential opportunity for me. I didn't hesitate to listen. He didn't know me, and I didn't know him, but after several meetings, he proposed an opportunity to run the company, and I jumped in with both feet.

Everyone thought I was crazy. Here I was working from home with no restrictions on my time, agreeing to run a start-up organization in a field I had no knowledge of that would require me to work full-time. This was exactly what I had said I *didn't* want with my previous work. But I recalled something that Thomas Edison had said. "Opportunity is missed by most people because it is dressed in overalls and looks like work." This was how this position appeared to others. But it didn't look that way to me. I knew this opportunity shouldn't be passed up even if it meant a little "hard work."

Life presents us with countless opportunities, and when they arise, we are faced with two options: 1) We can either seize them or 2) let fear hold us back and reject them. In my case, even though this opportunity seemed daunting, I had an inherent belief that I had the ability to achieve anything I set my mind to. I didn't have any self-perceived limitations, and I recognized this opportunity held the potential for growth. With unwavering determination, I embraced the position wholeheartedly, plunging into it headfirst.

"Sometimes, we are so attached to our way of life that we turn down wonderful opportunities simply because we don't know what to do with it." - Paulo Coelho

Opportunities serve as defining moments in our lives, shaping the paths we take and the stories we create. **Regret often stems from missed opportunities rather than the ones we pursued.** I look at opportunities as the universe's way of presenting avenues for fulfilling my desires and aligning with my future vision for my life. However, I'm also not naïve enough to believe that every opportunity that comes my way is automatically worth pursuing. I understand that there are both *good* opportunities and *bad* opportunities, and it's important to evaluate them thoroughly. Yes, throughout my journey I've missed a few *good* ones (especially in the stock market), but I've also dodged the bullet on a few bad ones. It's essential to carefully assess whether an opportunity resonates with your values, aspirations, and overall well-being before deciding to seize it.

When I looked at the opportunity of running a solar start-up, I listed all the pros and cons I could think of. To me, this was one way to quickly, and rationally determine whether it should be a go or no-go.

Every action you take and every choice you make holds the power to impact your life in some way. Whether it's a small decision or a significant life-altering choice, each one contributes to shaping your path and influencing your experience. Your choices have the potential to open new doors, create opportunities, and lead you toward personal growth. Conversely, they can also have unintended consequences or can steer you away from your desired outcomes. Recognizing the significance of your actions and choices empowers you to make deliberate decisions that align with your values and aspirations and ultimately shape the course of your life.

When contemplating important decisions, it's important to strike a balance between thoughtful analysis and timely action. While it's essential not to rush into hasty decisions without careful consideration, it's equally important to avoid prolonged deliberation that might cause missed opportunities. Acting impulsively without sufficient evaluation can lead to regrettable outcomes. Taking time to gather information and weighing the pros and cons can create a more informed decision-making process. Yet in saying that, overthinking or delaying decisions can also be detrimental. Opportunities often have time-sensitive aspects, and excessive hesitation may result in missed chances.

Some of you may recall this old parable: A man is at his home while the floodwaters rise into his house. Someone drives to his home and offers him a car ride to safety. He declines stating that God will save him. Then the waters rise higher, and the man makes his way to the second-story floor of his house. A man in a boat comes by and offers to bring him to safety. He declines stating that God will save him. Finally, the water has risen to the point where he must seek safety on the roof of his house. A helicopter flies down and offers to bring him to safety. Again, he declines. Eventually, the man is consumed by the flood and drowns. At the pearly gates, he asks God why he didn't save him. God replied, "I sent a car, a boat, and a helicopter, but you refused them all!"

This parable isn't about whether you believe in God or are religious. It is simply a story of missed opportunities. Opportunities are all around us, but there may be times when you can't see them as opportunities, wait too long to say yes, or are altogether too afraid to act on them. Can you think of a time when you may have missed an opportunity? How would it have changed your life if you hadn't missed it?

Even if you miss a good opportunity, however, you can't dwell on it or let it define you. Instead, stay positive and create a plan for the next time one crosses your path. I try to always be prepared and set the stage for potential opportunities to appear. Because I believe opportunities are all around us, I like to ask others about their work and what's going on that they're excited about. I like to talk to people in the airport, or while waiting in lines. I go to lunch by myself most days and eat at the bar. I'm thrilled to find someone interesting to talk to for a few minutes.

If I hadn't talked to the gentleman in line at FedEx, I wouldn't have ended up owning a solar energy company for the past fifteen years. Though I was brought in to run the business as a minority owner, within just a few short years I ended up owning 100% of the company, building it to a multi-million-dollar company, and then being named one of *Inc Magazines'* Fastest Growing Private Companies in America. Yes, I worked hard, and I was in the office most days from 7 a.m. to 7 p.m. in the beginning. But it didn't take long before I was setting my own schedule, playing tennis a few mornings each week, and still building the company.

As I have said before, I think that you and I can do anything that we believe we can. We just must give ourselves the chance to do it. Trust me,

I'm not extraordinary. There are people far more intelligent than I am, who are harder workers, who have more financial resources, and who have more inner drive. I was just smart enough to **watch for an opportunity, vet it when it was presented, deem it favorable, and seize it!**

Vetting opportunities are crucial. It's important not to blindly pursue every random opportunity that presents itself. You must have a clear vision of the future you desire for your life so that when you assess an opportunity, you can make sure it aligns with your values, goals, and vision. Then, you can determine if it will bring you closer to your envisioned life. Sometimes there will be opportunities you shouldn't take, but typically you'll know if it's not for you. Trust your gut! But then again, when you feel like it's the right choice for you – don't delay.

You can continue living your life where you are currently – maybe it's your comfort zone. And that might be an okay place for you. If so, fine. But if your dreams for your life are greater than where you are presently, then it means something needs to change. The action of seizing an opportunity can be filled with fraught and risk, which can be scary. And if you wait for perfect conditions, you may end up waiting forever.

So, ask yourself, "What ONE opportunity could change my life?"

Be a magnet that draws that opportunity to you. Bruce Lee embraced a powerful philosophy: "To hell with circumstances; I create opportunities." **Develop a visionary mindset that sees opportunities or creates them.** As Frances Bacon wisely proclaimed, "A wise man will make more opportunities than he finds." Strive to embody that wisdom and be that person. Embracing this mindset may initially push you beyond your comfort zone, but in hindsight, you might realize that a single choice, a chance taken, or an opportunity seized paved the way for everything you desired.

HOLD YOURSELF
RESPONSIBLE FOR YOUR
Results

Only You Can Get You to Where You Want to Go.

"You are accountable for your actions, your decisions, your life; no one else is, but you."

Catherine Pulsifer

In recent years, a prevalent trend in our society has been the tendency to place blame on others rather than take personal responsibility. This constant mantra of attributing fault has become pervasive. Whether it's blaming the Republicans, the Democrats, the government, your parents, the educational system, or your employer, the list goes on and on. It seems that finding someone to hold accountable has become the default response, perpetuating a culture of shifting responsibility.

Embracing the role of a successful She-EO entails accepting responsibility for your life, acknowledging your past actions and choices, and charting a path toward your future. Blaming others and external circumstances only hinders your progress and perpetuates a sense of victimhood. **Your life is ultimately NO ONE's fault but your own!** You are responsible for your decisions and choices, behaviors and actions, and your thoughts and attitude. It's these factors that determine your life situation. Yes, there are times when there are some outside factors, such as governmental rules that may make your situation more difficult, but it doesn't determine how you respond to it.

Being in a state of victimization is not the same as being a victim. A victim is someone who has been harmed or injured, either physically or emotionally. Being in a state of victimization, on the other hand, is a **mindset** of being harmed or injured. People who are in a state of victimization reflect the mindset of feeling helpless, powerless, and hopeless. They may believe that they are being targeted or picked on, and they may believe the unsatisfactory circumstances they find themselves in are due to the actions of others.

While it is easy and sometimes natural to blame external factors when facing less-than-ideal situations, it's important to recognize that your situation and mindset are not the fault of others. Taking responsibility for your actions in life is essential. We must acknowledge that while external factors may have influenced our circumstances, we have the power to shape our destinies. By assuming ownership of our lives, we can break free from the state of victimization and actively work toward creating a more empowered existence.

At one point in my career, it seemed that my employees were making regular costly mistakes. I blamed the crew leader for not doing quality checks and for not properly training the crew. It was easy to find someone to blame, and he was front and center. But in the end, when I analyzed the situation, I found that I moved this man into a position that he wasn't trained or capable of doing. I set him up for failure. Once I realized it was my mistake, I was able to move him into a position where he could succeed. I then placed a qualified individual into the role of crew leader, which resolved the issues. I had to trace the mistakes – and ultimately, it ended up with me.

It's important to remember that **making mistakes is a natural part of being human.** The key lies in acknowledging these mistakes. When you make a mistake, resist the temptation to make excuses or shift the blame to someone else. Instead, take full responsibility for your actions and learn from the mistakes and move on. It can be tempting to deceive yourself and place blame on external factors or other individuals. Instead, be honest with yourself and embrace responsibility. Holding yourself accountable for your actions, thoughts, and decisions enables personal growth and development, resilience, and training for future journeys.

Break free from the cycle of blame and adopt a responsible mindset that transcends limitations.

There are many benefits to taking accountability for your life. Here are a few:

- Increased self-esteem. When you take responsibility for your actions, you start to see yourself as someone capable and in control. This can lead to increased self-esteem and confidence.

- Improved relationships. When you are accountable for your actions, it builds trust and respect with others. This can lead to stronger and more fulfilling relationships.

- Elimination of a façade of perfection. It's tough to pretend to be perfect all the time. By eliminating the façade of perfection, it can reduce stress tremendously.

- Greater success. When you take responsibility for your goals, you are more likely to achieve them. This is because you are more likely to put in the effort and stay on track.

- Reduced stress. When you don't have to worry about blaming others for your problems, you can relax and focus on solutions. This can lead to a reduction in stress and anxiety.

- Increased happiness. When you are in control of your life and you are taking responsibility for your actions, you typically experience more happiness. This is because you are more likely to be living a life that is true to yourself and your values.

- Creates a team that takes ownership. You set an example for those around you. When you are accountable, it helps teach others to take ownership of their actions and thoughts, and it builds stronger bonds of trust.

- Encourages more emotionally intelligent conversations, thoughts, and interactions.

Accountability is a transformative force that holds the potential to create significant positive change. Although it may seem straightforward, the act of taking responsibility for our actions and decisions has the power to shape our lives in meaningful ways.

When we hold ourselves accountable, we become active participants in our own journey. We acknowledge our role in shaping our circumstances and outcomes, empowering ourselves to make intentional choices aligned with our values and goals. Accountability also fosters personal growth and development by enabling us to learn from our mistakes, make necessary adjustments, and strive for continuous improvement. It instills discipline, integrity, and commitment to excellence, fostering a sense of trust and reliability in our relationships and endeavors. By embracing this simple, yet powerful change, we create a positive ripple effect in our lives and the world around us.

When we blame others for our circumstances, however, we relinquish our power to take control of our lives. Blaming others shifts the responsibility away from ourselves and hinders our personal growth and development.

Instead of focusing on what we can do to improve our situation, we remain stuck in a cycle of pointing fingers.

Blaming others can lead to a mindset of helplessness, where we believe that our circumstances and life are entirely out of our control. This mindset is extremely harmful because it prevents us from seeking solutions or taking necessary steps to change the situation. It becomes a self-defeating attitude that has no upside.

Instead, adopt a mindset of self-accountability and holding yourself responsible. **By acknowledging your role in creating the circumstances of your life, you empower yourself to make changes and learn from your experiences.** Taking responsibility allows you to identify areas for personal growth, develop resilience, and find constructive ways to address challenges. It enables you to become a proactive problem-solver rather than a passive victim. This ultimately leads to greater self-confidence and a true sense of control over your life.

Reaching this critical juncture marks a significant turning point where the need to blame others diminishes, and the act of self-awareness helps you recognize and accept *your* role in shaping your life. As responsibility takes precedence, it propels you toward a path of self-empowerment. No longer confined by the limitations of blame, you can forge ahead with confidence to create the life you desire.

INTEGRITY AND BUILDING A PERSONAL CULTURE TO *Live By*

Create a Life that Represents the Best Version of You.

"Integrity is doing the right thing,
even when no one is watching."

C.S. Lewis

Integrity is a key component of building a strong personal culture to live by. It's the quality of being honest, trustworthy, and having strong moral principles. When you are living with integrity, you do what you believe is right, even when it's difficult.

When I entered what I called my second phase of life and moved into the solar industry, I was confronted with a strong lesson in integrity. Call me naïve, but I believed that most people were honest and had a moral compass to live their lives by. I quickly learned this wasn't the case.

Albert Einstein once said, "Whoever is careless with the truth in small matters cannot be trusted with important matters." After having finally acquired 100% of the company, it became evident to me that certain things weren't adding up. My lead technicians were given the ability to charge equipment and products necessary at Home Depot to complete repairs and installations. Most items were clear-cut and straightforward, and there didn't appear to be any red flags. Then it seemed each month there were one or two items that I questioned but were quickly explained away by a certain technician. It wasn't until three months later when I received a bill for almost fifteen thousand dollars of miscellaneous tools that I halted all action and froze the account.

All technicians pleaded not guilty to charging any of these items to my account, so I studied the signature of the signor for days until I finally noticed one small similarity to one of my technician's handwritings. Long story short, this tech was buying items on my Home Depot account and then pawning them at a local pawn shop. This was easily proven because the pawn shop required a driver's license. He was immediately let go, and due to several similar previous offenses, he had to confront his dishonesty.

Being honest is a critical part of building a personal culture to live by.

There are many benefits to having integrity. First, you don't have to keep track of your lies. **People with integrity are more likely to be successful in their personal and professional lives.** Being truthful is an asset that helps to build strong relationships, live a more fulfilling life, and be happy.

Integrity encompasses not only the quality of our words but also the actions we take. You may have heard the saying, **"You are what you do, not what you say you will do."** We are all familiar with those individuals who promise the world but fail to follow through. It may be something as simple as promising to take your child to the park but continually putting it off. **Integrity hinges on the alignment between words, promises, and actions.** There must be a consistency of actions. Yes, there will be times in life when this is impossible, but when it happens, take ownership and responsibility.

As Katrina Mayer aptly stated, "Integrity is making sure that the things you say and the things you do are in alignment." It's like telling your child never to drink and smoke while you indulge in both habits at home. Such actions contradict your words and erode respect and trust. Integrity flourishes when our words and actions align, fostering trust, credibility, and meaningful connections. It's important to strive for consistency and accountability, openly acknowledging any deviations and working toward rectifying them.

Also, being kind is a key factor in developing a culture to live by. It doesn't matter how rich, poor, educated, popular, or not popular someone might be, treating them all with kindness, respect, and significance helps them to feel important. **When you shine a light on others, you are seen as a person of integrity.** Mother Teresa exemplifies such as individual. She dedicated herself to spending time with the most unloved, ill, and destitute and treated them with unwavering compassion as if they were the most important people in the world. Her acts of kindness surpassed all measures of love.

I've encountered individuals who present themselves one way to those they perceive as superior or who they believe can benefit them, but then display a complete lack of respect and mistreatment toward employees or waitstaff. Witnessing such behavior leaves me with a profound sense of distaste in my mouth. I find it challenging to respect individuals who exhibit such inconsistency, because, in my view, it reflects a lack of integrity. I firmly believe in treating everyone with kindness and respect, regardless of their status or position and even when you have nothing to gain from them. Upholding this principle is essential to fostering true integrity. **Treat everyone well.**

Building a personal culture of integrity starts with understanding what is important to you. What are your core values? What do you believe in? Once you know what is important to you, you can start to make choices that align with those values.

Here are some tips for building a personal culture of integrity:

- Be honest with yourself. This means being honest about your strengths, weaknesses, goals, and dreams. When you are honest with yourself, you can start to make changes that will help you live a more fulfilling life.

- Be honest with others. This means being truthful, even when it is difficult. It also means being fair and just. When you are honest with others, you build trust and respect.

- Stand up for what you believe in. Even when it is difficult, it is important to stand up for what you believe in. This shows that you have integrity and that you are willing to fight for what you believe in.

- Do what you say you will do. It's important to try to be true to your word. Try not to make promises you know you can't keep.

- Be kind to others. Everyone is important no matter their status in life. It is important to be kind to others, even when you have no reason to be. This shows that you have compassion and the ability to make everyone feel important.

Cultivating a personal culture of integrity is a process that demands dedication and commitment. It requires consistently aligning your actions, values, and principles. Although it may take time and effort, investing in developing integrity is incredibly rewarding.

Integrity serves as a guiding compass that shapes your interactions, decisions, and relationships. When you embody integrity, you build a solid foundation of trust and authenticity. Others perceive you as reliable, and your words carry weight. Deeper bonds and connections are fostered, which brings a sense of inner peace and harmony. You can navigate life with clarity and conviction, knowing that you are staying true to yourself and your principles.

In essence, developing a personal culture to live by and having integrity is not only a worthwhile investment but also an essential component of a fulfilling and meaningful life. By embodying integrity, you create a life that is rooted in authenticity, trust, and personal growth, paving the way for your success and lasting happiness.

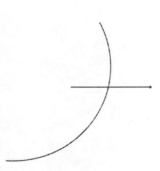

17

IT'S NOT ALWAYS SUNSHINE AND *Roses*

Adversity Can Strike
Us All. It's How We
React to it That
Matters.

"The tiny seed knew that in order to grow, it needed to be dropped in dirt, covered with darkness, and struggle to reach the light."

Sandra Kring

Henry Ford once said, "When everything seems to be going against you, remember that the airplane takes off against the wind, not with it." Life won't always be sunshine and roses. Considering what has been discussed so far, it may seem that the advice presented is easy if everything goes your way; but what about when it does not?

I've never come across a single individual who has lived a life where everything went his or her way 100% of the time. Adversity, setbacks, and difficulties are part of the human experience. In life and business, there will be challenges that are thrown in your path, but if you're smart, you can skirt around, climb over, and even push through most of them. For those times when this is impossible, it's all about your attitude and mindset.

When adversity, challenges, or difficulties (ACD) strike, there are three things you can do:

1) Let it define you.

2) Let it consume and ultimately destroy you.

3) Let it strengthen you.

Life doesn't always unfold according to our plans, and there are moments when it seems like everything is going smoothly. However, just when we least expect it, unforeseen circumstances or challenges can suddenly arise, metaphorically likened to a bolt of lightning. You can't plan for every scenario, but trust me, I often try. I'm organized, a planner, and most of the time think I'm in control of my life. But from time to time, I'm hit with thirty thousand volts of electricity which shows me that ultimately, I don't have the control I think I have. During such moments, I find myself needing **to tap into the depths of my inner strength and resilience.** I push myself to remain standing and continue moving forward, regardless of the difficulties I face.

In a tragic accident a few years ago, my family lost our seventeen-month-old granddaughter. At that moment, our lives came to a halt, and nothing held any importance other than helping and supporting our family through this devastating event. This was a horrific experience and one that many never recover from. It could have consumed and destroyed our family, but we chose to **transform it into a source of strength.**

Despite the overwhelming grief we experienced, we also had the responsibility to continue living for the sake of our then-five-year-old granddaughter. This responsibility served as a driving force that enabled us to approach each day one step at a time, putting one foot in front of the other, as we navigated through the healing process. Then, as another step in our healing, we established a non-profit organization, Kit's Kindness, in honor of our beloved Kit.

In life, we all encounter obstacles and challenges on occasion. However, when we face genuine adversity, it has the power to stop us in our tracks. I'm sure you all have a story of heartache, tragedy, failure, or difficulty. It may have been a divorce, a life-threatening illness, a death, or the failure of a business. All these tribulations can halt your progress, make you want to crawl into bed, want to pull the covers over your head and make you feel completely immobilized.

There are no words or actions that I can give you that will magically resolve all difficulties and make everything "all better" instantly. It's up to you, and you alone, to face these situations daily, try to survive them, and eventually overcome them or learn to live with them. The Greek philosopher Herodotus said, "Adversity has the effect of drawing out strength and qualities of a man that would have lain dormant or absent." It is also often said that you will not be given more than you can handle. If this holds true, then it implies that **we possess within us the strength and qualities necessary to confront and overcome any challenge that comes our way.**

Though there is no one-size script for this, I can tell you with almost utmost certainty that the key to overcoming adversity and those difficult days is by taking as many of these steps as you can.

1. React calmly and rationally.
2. Confront the situation realistically without blowing it out of proportion.
3. Brainstorm solutions if any.
4. Manage intense emotions such as anxiety, fear, or grief.
5. Breathe deeply.
6. Try to remain calm.
7. Accept the situation.
8. Find ways to maintain a sense of normalcy.
9. Seek support from friends, family, and professional counselors if necessary.
10. Invest in self-care. (Improve sleep, eat well, exercise.)
11. Believe in yourself and your ability to make it through the storm.
12. Give it time.
13. Stay active and productive.
14. Choose to survive it.

15. Create positive reactions and emotions toward the situation as best you can. When a negative thought arises, try to counter it with a more positive one.

16. Look for meaning and purpose.

17. Become mentally tough.

18. Be kind to yourself.

19. Either overcome it, accept it, or learn to live with it.

Life is a journey of unpredictable twists and turns, often void of sunshine and roses. Along this path, we encounter adversity, challenges, and hardships that test our resilience, strength, and character. While it may be tempting to yearn for a life without difficulties, it is in facing them that we grow, learn, and discover the depths of our inner strength.

Adversity is an inherent part of the human experience. No one is exempt from its grasp, regardless of age, background, or status. It arrives unannounced, disrupting our plans and forcing us to confront our vulnerabilities. It shakes our confidence and pushes us to boundaries never crossed. The quote by Dieter F. Uchtdorf reminds us, however, "That it's **our response to adversity, rather than the adversity itself, that shapes the course of our life's journey.**" It is our reactions and choices that determine how we grow and develop. It's through these challenging times that resilience becomes our lifeline. It's the ability to bounce back, adapt, and persevere.

Though the death of a loved one is an experience that can never be *bounced back* from or forgotten, it quickly becomes a part of our lives. We learn to live with the pain and grief every single day, and we bear these scars for a lifetime. Yet, as time passes, we slowly transform these wounds into wisdom.

I believe that the best of us turn our wounds into wisdom and growth. Martin Luther King, Jr. believed that "The ultimate measure of a man is not where he stands in moments of comfort and convenience, but where he stands at times of challenge and controversy." During challenging times, our true strength is put to the test. It's in these moments, however, that we need to embrace our wounds and the hidden lessons within the storm. The lessons learned through pain and hardship have the power to shape our character and guide us toward a more enlightened path.

Remember, it's not the absence of challenges that defines our character, but rather our ability to face them. By doing this, we cultivate wisdom, deepen our understanding of ourselves, and emerge stronger than before.

I pray you never have to experience a loss such as our family did. In times of great sorrow and adversity, you can feel incredibly isolated and as if no one else could comprehend the weight of your pain. However, it's important to remember that you are not alone in your suffering. Countless individuals have faced their own trials, and grief and pain cannot be neatly packaged, compared, or resolved quickly. The process of healing takes time, and everyone's journey is unique. But I promise, with time and endurance, it will be possible to envision a brighter future once again.

18

HELP OTHERS AND
Give Back

*Giving is a Privilege
Not a Duty.*

"Life's most persistent and urgent question is, what are you doing for others?"

Martin Luther King Jr.

No matter what your personal circumstances are, there are always opportunities to help others and contribute to their well-being. It's a common misconception that assistance requires financial wealth. **Acts of kindness do not always involve money.** They can be as simple as dedicating your time, helping others, or sharing a warm smile. Dolly Parton once wisely remarked, "If you see someone without a smile today, give 'em yours." Smiles hold remarkable power. We often underestimate the impact of a genuine smile, a kind word, a heartfelt compliment, or any small act that shows care and compassion. These gestures can make a world of difference to someone in need.

There have been times in my life that have been filled with immense blessings, while at other times, I faced profound tragedies. On those occasions when everything was going well for me, finances were abundant, and life was good, it was easy to donate to causes, volunteer my time, and smile and be kind to those around me. It was easy to help others and give back to the community. I think many of us can relate to this. But in times of difficulty, it's often hard to see beyond our noses, let alone help others. It's in these times we must pull back the curtain and face the light to attempt to see beyond our situation to the needs of others.

As I mentioned earlier, the loss of my granddaughter completely altered my world. In the wake of this tragedy, everything seemed insignificant and devoid of meaning. Nothing else mattered, nothing held any purpose, and I found myself mired in grief, self-pity, and pain. I don't begin to compare the depths of my sorrow to my daughter's, but it was she who taught me how to rise by helping others and giving something back.

As my granddaughter's birthday approached, my daughter wanted to do something in honor of her memory. She and her husband decided to perform a random act of kindness each day for a week and asked their friends and family to do the same. They wanted to bring happiness to others during a grief-filled time for them. Everyone came through, and the week was so successful, and so many acts of kindness were performed, that the following year on what would have been Kit's third birthday, her parents decided to officially declare the date, Kit's Kindness Day, and ask everyone to perform random acts of kindness once again. Friends, family, and even strangers made Kit's Kindness Day a huge success by performing random acts of kindness across the United States.

We were so overwhelmed by how many people participated that we decided we should not limit Kit's Kindness to only one day a year. It was then we started the process of turning Kit's Kindness into a nonprofit charitable organization so we could help children and others throughout the year.

Kit's Kindness is now a 501(c)3 non-profit organization that helps children and families in need. We promote children's health, safety, education, and mental well-being. We also continue to celebrate our beloved little girl's birthday with Kit's Kindness Day as we perform random acts of kindness and ask others to do the same.

Despite the lasting pain of losing Kit, we learned that by reaching out to help others and taking action to give back to our community, we not only helped the recipient but also experienced a sense of inner personal satisfaction. **Engaging in acts of kindness gives us a sense of purpose and connection to something greater than ourselves.**

As we immersed ourselves in our non-profit organization, we encountered stories that affirmed the significance of our efforts. Unbeknownst to us, our act of reaching out to a young mother who had recently lost her baby to SIDS inadvertently prevented her from taking her own life. We had no inkling of the profound impact our kindness and support would have on her, but it did. This experience, and many more like it served as a touching reminder of the ripple effects that acts of kindness can have in someone's life, even when we are unaware of the magnitude of our impact.

Extensive research has shown that individuals who engage in helping others and giving back are happier and more satisfied with their lives. By extending a helping hand, we establish meaningful connections with others and develop a greater sense of purpose in the world. These acts of kindness serve as a reminder of our interconnectedness and ability to make a positive impact on others. Therefore, these **acts of kindness are not solely altruistic; they are also a pathway to your personal happiness.**

There are numerous ways you can help others and give back to your community. Here are some opportunities to consider:

- Volunteer your time.
- Find a charity that supports causes you care about.
- Donate food to a food bank.
- Adopt a pet from a shelter.
- Become a mentor to a child.
- Help at a soup kitchen or homeless shelter.
- Donate funds to a charitable cause.
- Tutor a child.
- Donate blood.

- Organize or participate in fundraising activities to support your favorite charity.

- Plant a tree.

- Donate no longer used clothing to shelters.

- Spend time with nursing home residents.

- Support local businesses.

- Offer your professional skills to non-profits.

- Or simply be kind and compassionate toward others.

Giving encompasses the willingness to be present, lend support, and show empathy. It doesn't always have to involve grand gestures or financial resources. **Even small acts of kindness and everyday generosity can make a significant impact on someone's life.** By selecting opportunities that align with your interests, values, and the time you can commit, you can find the right path to giving back. When you adopt an open mindset, altruistic opportunities will become more visible, allowing you to make a difference in the world.

So, keep in mind, during both the highs and lows of life, we can find ways to help others. When we are experiencing success and abundance, it's a natural inclination to think about how we can assist those in need. However, it's equally important, if not more so, to extend our kindness and support during challenging moments.

When we are facing difficulties, it can be easy to become consumed by our own struggles, yet it is precisely during these times that our acts of compassion and assistance may hold even more power. It allows us to shift our mindset from our adversity to the needs of others around us. This act of selflessness not only provides support to others but also allows us to gain a fresh perspective on our challenges and reminds us that we are not alone in our struggles.

"I've learned that you shouldn't go through life with a catcher's mitt on both hands. You need to be able to throw something back." — Maya Angelou

Embrace the power you hold to make a positive difference, for everything you do matters.

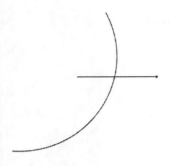

19

BE
Persistent

Your Actions Define Your Life More Than Circumstances Do.

"Keep Going. Your hardest times often lead to the greatest moments of your life. Keep going. Tough situations build strong people in the end."

Roy T. Bennett

Before losing my granddaughter, my daughter and son-in-law worked in the business with me. Working together with my family gave me a sense of purpose to build a company that would be passed down to future generations. After the accident, however, neither of them could return to work. So now I was not only coupled with the loss of my granddaughter but the absence of my daughter and son-in-law in the business as well. This created a void that seemed insurmountable, which made it difficult for me to return.

For the next several months, my employees stepped up, displaying their dedication and commitment to the company. They delivered work to me in the mornings by dropping it off on my doorstep and would pick it up at the end of the day in the same manner. They became the pillars that held the business together, ensuring its continuity in the face of adversity. Their unwavering support and willingness to take on new responsibilities highlighted the strength of our team and the shared sense of purpose that drove us all forward.

But there came a pivotal moment when I knew it was time to step back into the office and face the void that had been left behind. It was a task that carried the weight of grief and the pressure of revitalizing the dreams I once had for the company.

Persistence is the ability to keep going, even when things are tough. It's the fuel that propels you forward when everything else tells you to give up. It's the willingness to keep trying, even when you fail. And it's the unwavering faith in yourself, and the refusal to accept defeat as the outcome.

There are many reasons why persistence is important. First, it helps us to overcome obstacles. When we are persistent, we are more likely to find a way to overcome the challenges that we face. Second, persistence helps us to achieve our goals. If we give up easily, we will never reach our full potential. Third, persistence helps us to build character. When we are persistent, we learn to persevere through difficult times. This makes us stronger and more resilient.

But what exactly is persistence? It's not a mere act of stubbornness or blind determination. **Persistence is a combination of resilience, patience, and**

adaptability. It's the ability to stay focused on a goal while navigating the ever-changing landscape of challenges and setbacks.

At its core, persistence is a mindset—an unshakable belief in your ability to overcome any obstacle. It is the realization that failure is not a reflection of your worth but a stepping-stone on the path to success. In the face of failure, the persistent individual rises, dusts off the disappointment, learns from the experience, and turns setbacks into opportunities for growth.

There are many examples of people who have achieved great things through persistence. Helen Keller was blind and deaf, but she became a successful author and lecturer. Nelson Mandela was imprisoned for twenty-seven years, but he eventually became the president of South Africa. And Malala Yousafzai was shot by the Taliban for speaking out for girls' education, but she has since become a Nobel Prize winner and an advocate for education around the world.

The road to achievement is often winding and treacherous. It tests our resolve, challenges our abilities, and demands unwavering dedication. It is during these times of uncertainty that the true power of persistence reveals itself. It is with relentless determination that even the most arduous tasks can be overcome.

But persistence is not just a solitary endeavor; it thrives within a community of support and encouragement as it did within my business.

Surrounding yourself with individuals who believe in you and what you are trying to achieve can be what helps you to move forward. Together, they lift you up during moments of doubt, celebrate each other's victories, and provide the unwavering support needed to overcome the toughest of challenges. I was thankful I had these types of people in my life and business.

Throughout life, there will be moments when the weight of adversity threatens to crush our spirits. It's during these moments that we must draw strength from within and remind ourselves of our purpose. We must remember that happiness, fulfillment, and success rarely come without their fair share of difficulties and that every setback is an opportunity to rise stronger and wiser.

The path of persistence may be tough and challenging, filled with obstacles and setbacks, but the rewards it offers are truly immeasurable. It's through persistence that ordinary individuals have achieved extraordinary feats, that groundbreaking discoveries have been made, and that seemingly impossible dreams have been realized. Many of humanity's greatest achievements can be traced back to individuals who refused to give up in the face of seemingly insurmountable challenges. The stories of those who have turned once-impossible dreams into reality through sheer persistence serve as a testament to the human spirit's incredible capacity for resilience and determination.

While the path of persistence may be arduous and filled with uncertainty, it's precisely this tenacity that separates those who achieve greatness from those who abandon their dreams.

As you journey through life, embrace the unyielding mindset of persistence. Commit yourself to the pursuit of your dreams, armed with unwavering determination and an unbreakable spirit. And in doing so, discover the boundless possibilities that lie beyond the realm of what is known, for it is in persistence that we unlock our true potential.

So how do you develop persistence? **Don't give up.**

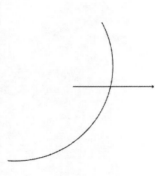

INSPIRATION AND TRUSTING IN THE *Universe*

Tap Into Your Inspiration and Let the Magic Unfold.

*"The universe is not outside of you. Look inside
yourself; everything that you want, you already are."*
Rumi

As a young girl, I would often venture into the woods to play with my imaginary fairy friends. I believed they communicated with me through the rustling of the leaves, the crackling of the forest floor underfoot, and the symphony of bird and animal calls. During my solitary moments in the forest, I found that most of my thoughts and questions received answers. Today, if I can quiet my mind enough, I can still perceive that voice, but I now know it to be my inner voice (or intuition) instead of the fairies. It serves as a constant and reliable guide that is always with me and aids me in navigating my life.

The power of this voice often surpasses our underestimation. It isn't solely driven by logic or emotions, but it holds the potential to offer valuable guidance. Learn to attune yourself to it for it can provide inspired solutions to problems. It might trigger a "gut" feeling that leads to inner guidance, but it's also a source of creativity. In my case, this inner voice and inspiration are the origins of my books. Each fiction novel I've written has been inspired by dreams, the whimsical nature of the subconscious, or what some may refer to as their inner muse. If you seek inspiration, don't wait for it to strike like lightning. Actively pursue it. Dedicate time to quiet your thoughts and listen. The answers will reveal themselves. Try to tap into that inner voice daily, and it will help guide you and your actions.

"The quieter you become, the more you hear." Ram Dass

Inspiration is a powerful force that resides within each of us, waiting to be awakened and harnessed. It's the spark that ignites our creativity, fuels our passions, and propels us toward the fulfillment of our dreams. We all have moments of inspiration. It could be a sudden flash of insight, a feeling of deep knowing, or a sense of being guided by something greater than ourselves. **When we tap into our inspiration, we connect with our true potential and create things that are both beautiful and meaningful.** But how do we tap into this wellspring of inspiration? How do we cultivate the trust necessary to believe in the universe's abundant support?

First, you must create some space for it in your life. Carve out moments of stillness and reflection. You don't have to meditate like a monk for hours. It can be as simple as a quiet walk in the woods or simply sitting in quiet contemplation. For me, I spend about ten minutes before falling asleep and ten minutes upon waking to listen to this inner voice. **When you can quiet the noise of the external world, it allows this voice to emerge whispering ideas, insights, and solutions into your ear.**

Trusting in the universe (*or inner self, higher power, God, or whatever word you might find most comfortable using)* is vital for unlocking inspiration. It involves surrendering your need for control and embracing the belief that there is a larger, interconnected web of forces at play. It means understanding that everything happens for a reason, even if we can't always see it in the present moment. It means letting go of doubt, fear, and limiting beliefs. It means facing challenges and setbacks with resilience, knowing that they are stepping stones on our path to growth and fulfillment. And it means stepping outside our comfort zones, taking risks, and embracing uncertainty.

When I let go, listen, and trust my inner voice and the universe, I seem to align myself with the flow of life, and suddenly, synchronicities unfold. Doors open, opportunities arise, and the right people and resources come into my life at precisely the right time. This forces me to acknowledge that we are not alone on this journey and that we are supported and guided by some unknown force that seeks our highest good. Ralph Waldo Emerson once wrote, "The universe is always conspiring for your good."

Trusting in the universe and tapping into inspiration go hand in hand. By surrendering to the creative process and allowing ideas to flow through us, we become vessels for something greater than ourselves. When we tap into our imagination, inspiration dances with our unique perspectives and experiences. It is in this union that we create works of art, write captivating stories, compose beautiful music, and bring forth innovations that shape the world. We also find solutions to problems and insight into our greater purpose in life.

It's vitally important for women to trust their instincts. It's often easy to let pressures from others sway our thinking; and it's sometimes easier to go along with the crowd, our business partners, or even our spouse. Be open to their opinions, but always listen to your inner self and believe whatever it's telling you. Trust the information that the universe is giving you, as it will always guide you in the right direction. Your intuition draws upon your experiences, values, and emotions, helping you to make decisions that align with your authentic self. Staying true to this is about finding the right balance between being receptive and trusting your own instincts.

When we open ourselves up to receiving guidance and support, we allow ourselves to be led by our intuition. We trust that the universe will provide us with everything we need to fulfill our purpose. "The universe is saying, 'Allow me to flow through you unrestricted, and you will see the greatest magic you have ever seen.'" – Klaus Joehle

So how do we tap into our inspiration and trust in the universe? Here are a few tips:

- **Get quiet.** One of the best ways to tap into your inspiration is to get quiet and listen to your inner voice.

- **Be open to new experiences.** When you're open to new experiences, you're more likely to be inspired. Try new things, meet new people, and explore new places.

- **Don't be afraid to fail.** Failure is a part of life, and it can be a good thing. Failure teaches us what doesn't work, and it helps us to grow and learn.

- **Believe in yourself.** The most important thing is to believe in yourself and your ability to create something beautiful. When you believe in yourself, you're more likely to take risks and follow your dreams.

Tapping into your inspiration and trusting in the universe is a journey, not a destination. It's a process of learning to listen to your inner voice, being open to new experiences, and trusting yourself. It's a journey that's well worth taking. When you listen to this small voice inside, you'll find you begin to create a life that is both fulfilling and meaningful.

Here are some additional tips for tapping into your inspiration:

- **Keep a journal.** Writing down your thoughts and feelings can help you to process your inspiration and make sense of it.

- **Talk to a trusted friend or therapist.** Sometimes, it can be helpful to talk to someone else about your inspiration. They can offer support and guidance.

- **Act.** The best way to bring your inspiration to life is to act. Don't be afraid to put your ideas into the world.

Create space for stillness. When you listen to your inner voice, believe in the interconnectedness of all things, and allow the universe to guide you, you open yourself up to where you unlock the boundless potential that resides within you. You will begin to see the world in a new way as inspired action flows from your heart and soul, and you live your most fulfilled life.

21

REVERSE ENGINEER YOUR

Success

Success Leaves Clues for You to Follow.

"If you want to be successful, find someone who has already achieved the results you want and model their behavior."

Tony Robbins

Reverse engineering is the process of looking at someone (or a business) that has achieved what you want to achieve, and then studying them (or it) to figure out how it came to be. If you can understand *how* someone achieved success, you can begin to recreate it and replicate it for your own life or business. As you deconstruct the achievements of others, you can examine their journey and the strategies they used to gain valuable insights and apply them to your own endeavors.

Some of the most successful businessmen, authors, artists, and inventors use reverse engineering to achieve their goals, look for inspiration, improve their performance, and achieve whatever it is they want to achieve. They often begin by finding examples that are worth analyzing. When Napolean Hill wrote, *Think and Grow Rich*, a book that sold over thirty million copies, he hadn't achieved success or wealth. In fact, he struggled financially for much of his early life. Yet, he spent twenty years researching and writing the book while interviewing over 500 successful and wealthy people, including Andrew Carnegie, Henry Ford, Thomas Edison, and John D. Rockefeller. He studied what these 500 people did to achieve success, and he used this information in a manner that reflected and enhanced his talent – writing. Once the book was released, it became an instant bestseller and made Hill a very wealthy man.

You can apply this technique to almost any area from wanting to build a successful business, to being a wonderful mother, to being a great athlete, to making the best-tasting cheesecake. You can read books, watch interviews, study YouTube videos, or talk to people. All help to be able to better understand their success. When you do this, you will also most likely begin to recognize the traits that make them distinctive over others, patterns, and commonalities.

What key factors contributed to their success? What opportunities did they take advantage of? What challenges did they overcome?

Once you have an idea of the above, you can begin to analyze their mindset and attitude. **Successful individuals often possess a growth mindset, believing that abilities and intelligence can be developed through dedication, hard work, and growth.** They embrace failure as an opportunity to learn, rather than see it as a setback. And by adopting a similar mindset, it will help you to persevere and achieve your goals. Study the traits and skills they have mastered and then score your abilities against them. This begins to give you a roadmap or path to move toward if you want to achieve similar results. As you incorporate the key factors they have into your own life or business, you'll see the changes you need to make, the skills you might need to develop, and the resources you need to acquire.

You can ask yourself questions like:

- What would be the final step you would need to take to reach your goal?
- Who has already achieved this?
- Can you study how they accomplished it?
- What skills would you need to have?
- What financial resources do you need?
- Whose help might you need?
- What actions would you need to take?
- What mindset do you have to adopt?
- Who do you have to become to reach that goal?

Though reverse engineering can help to provide valuable insights, it's not a guarantee of success. There is no one-size-fits-all formula, as everyone's journey is unique, and what works for someone else may not always work for you. However, **success does leave clues.** And if you follow those clues, you can learn from the experiences of others and can tailor this information to suit your own strengths, passions, and circumstances. You can avoid pitfalls and bypass mistakes. As Eleanor Roosevelt wisely stated, "Learn from the mistakes of others. You can't live long enough to make them all yourself."

Someone who has proven to be very successful at reverse engineering success is Elon Musk. When Tesla entered the electric vehicle market, Elon began by studying both the elements of success and failure of car manufacturers. Once identified, instead of trying to replicate what they did, he focused on high performance, longer ranges, and sleeker designs, which transformed the perception of electric vehicles.

I can relate to Musk's approach. He didn't try to replicate what others had already done. He studied them in order to do things differently and better. I found the need to do the same when I entered the solar industry. After coming from a highly regulated financial industry, I found myself in what I thought was the Wild West. It was an industry with very little regulation and controls, and oftentimes, questionable practices. My goal wasn't to replicate the success these other companies were having with their processes, my goal was to do things differently and create a gold standard that eventually the industry would need to follow. So, by studying what they were doing, I was given a starting point. From there I could change and adapt to processes that aligned more with my personal culture.

Let's also consider the example of understanding the workings of an electric lightbulb. If faced with the challenge, it would be wise to study the achievements of Thomas Edison. Rather than starting at the beginning as he did with countless failed attempts, you could immediately focus on the point where he succeeded.

By delving into the mindset, strategies, and actions of successful individuals, you gain invaluable insights to align with your specific circumstances and goals. This approach enables you to bypass unnecessary hurdles and accelerate your progress toward achieving your desired outcome. By following the clues left by successful individuals, you can extract valuable lessons and principles that resonate with your aspirations and goals. However, it's crucial to tailor the information you gather to your own circumstances and leverage your strengths and passions.

Reverse engineering can be valuable for women seeking to achieve success. Here are a few ways to apply reverse engineering:

1. Identify role models -- Look for successful women in your desired field or who have achieved the type of success or fulfillment you aspire to.
2. Study and analyze -- Study the strategies they employed and analyze the steps they took to reach their goals.

3. Define your vision -- Define what success means to you on a personal level. This will serve as your framework as you reverse engineer the path to your desired outcomes.

4. Learn from failures -- Analyze setbacks and challenges faced by successful women and understand how they overcame them.

5. Develop skills -- Identify the skills, knowledge, and expertise required to excel, and acquire the education, training, and experiences needed to build your foundation.

6. Build your network – Surround yourself with supportive and like-minded people.

By leveraging these basic principles of reverse engineering, you can gain valuable insights into your own version of success and fulfillment. Yet, keep in mind that ultimately, everyone's journey is unique. While there is immense value in studying the experiences of successful individuals, it's important to adapt their insight to your own personal circumstances. By following the clues they left behind, you can accelerate your personal growth, minimize setbacks, and forge a path that aligns with your goals and passions.

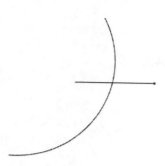

CONFIDENCE AND FEMININE *Power*

Use the Gifts and Abilities You Were Born With.

"Feminine power isn't something we go out and acquire; it's already within us."

Marianne Williamson

Learning to harness and embrace your feminine power is not about imitating or replicating the success of men; it's about forging your unique path. It requires a deep understanding and unwavering belief in yourself, refusing to adopt others' opinions without first examining them for yourself. It involves trusting your instincts and actions, without constantly second-guessing yourself. Most importantly, it entails possessing enough confidence in your own identity that you don't feel compelled to follow the crowd or emulate others.

As humans, **we possess both feminine and masculine energies,** which represent contrasting aspects of our being. **Achieving a fulfilling life involves striking the right balance between these energies.** Masculine energy is often associated with aggressiveness, logical thinking, determination, confidence, and a results-oriented mindset. On the other hand, feminine energy is characterized by compassion, kindness, creativity, intuition, nurturing, and an inclination toward emotional expression.

Masculine energy tends to be more structured and rigid, while feminine energy flows more naturally and organically.

The question is: which energy holds the key to unlocking the success you desire? Conventional wisdom might suggest that masculine energy is more closely linked to achievement. However, embracing and harnessing the power of feminine energy can also propel you to great heights. Many women in the business world feel compelled to suppress their feminine side to appear more in control and competent. However, a truly confident woman understands that by honoring her innate qualities and allowing them to guide her, she can unleash even greater power and attain remarkable respect and success.

By utilizing your feminine energy, you tap into a fountain of this quieter power. It enables you to cultivate empathy, compassion, and emotional intelligence, which are essential for building meaningful connections and a successful life. The creative force within feminine energy fuels innovation and allows for thinking outside the box, leading to fresh perspectives, and groundbreaking ideas. Intuition becomes a guiding force, helping you make sound decisions and navigate through uncertainty with grace. Nurturing tendencies empower you to support and uplift those around you, creating an environment conducive to growth and collaboration.

Throughout my professional journey, I have consciously chosen my own techniques and approaches to conducting business and interacting with others. I've allowed my feminine side to play a pivotal role in how I interact in business. As a result, I've stayed true to my innate qualities, which has allowed me to be the best I can be without trying to be something I'm not.

Contrary to the misconception that feminine qualities are a sign of weakness, when used effectively, they can drive you toward success and fulfillment. It grants you the ability to approach challenges with resilience and grace, adapting to changing circumstances, and finding solutions in unconventional ways. By embracing and embodying your authentic self, you become a role model and inspiration to others, forging a path that celebrates and validates the power of femininity.

Initially, the males in my industry were uncertain of how to interact with me, leading to frequent awkward encounters. I recall being fortunate enough to participate in an annual trip organized by one of my distributors as a bonus for their highest-performing producers. On numerous occasions, fellow top producers would approach my male partner, extend a handshake, and engage in a business-related conversation. He would quickly clarify that he wasn't in the solar business and that it was, in fact, my business. This revelation often resulted in an awkward pause, followed by a hesitant "oh", and then they moved on. Nevertheless, as the years went by, I fostered pivotal relationships and earned their respect and support by continually achieving the honor to attend these events, as well as staying true to my authentic self.

I had no intention of conforming to the archetype of the "good ol' boys", and I didn't seek membership into their exclusive club. Nor did I feel the need to. I engaged and interacted when necessary or appropriate, but I didn't feel compelled to push myself into their club, where both of us may have felt ingenuine. Instead, I embraced my feminine side and pursued my own path while standing true to my individuality. I believe it allowed me to bring a unique perspective to the male-dominated industry I was in and contribute in meaningful ways without sacrificing or changing who I was. Using the gift of your feminine power is about embracing your unique strengths and being unapologetically true to yourself. By striking the right balance between feminine and masculine energies, you unlock your full potential, propelling yourself toward achievement.

I have achieved personal and professional successes on my terms. I forged my own unconventional path guided by my intuition and deep belief in the power of authenticity. In my journey, I've challenged paradigms and discovered the extraordinary power that **being yourself is – one of the most powerful traits you can possess.**

Embracing your uniqueness allows you to unleash your full potential and contribute your distinct perspective to the world. Remember that your true worth, however, comes from within, not from external validation. Celebrate your achievements, acknowledge your growth, and be compassionate with yourself during challenging times. Stay true to yourself and cultivate a strong sense of perfection that lies in being the individual you were born to be.

23

FEELING *Worthy*

You are Worthy of Everything You Desire.

"Our sense of self-worth is the single most important determinant of the health, abundance, and joy we allow into our lives."

Dan Millman

Women often struggle when it comes to feeling worthy of the things that they desire or achieve. Due to the subjective nature of self-worth, it's found that women tend to be more self-critical, making it challenging to grant themselves a sense of being deserving or feeling worthy. However, it's important to understand that worthiness is not dependent on external achievements or societal validations. It's derived from existence itself. **Worthiness does not result from what you do or have done but is simply gained because of who you *are*.**

Feeling unworthy can stem from comparing our perceived worth to that of others. You might compare in areas of appearance, financial wealth, what you do, what you have achieved, or even what your social media following is. When you take a yardstick and start measuring your achievements against another, you can shortchange your own abilities and qualities while focusing on theirs. This can quickly make you doubt yourself and question your worth.

Also, feeling unworthy can stem from the belief that to deserve worthiness, your actions, results, and *you* must be perfect. This is another misconception that many women hold. As someone who can relate to the desire of pursuing perfectionism, I understand the dissatisfaction that arises when results fall short, affecting our sense of self-worth. However, I have learned to embrace my imperfections, liberating myself from the shackles of perfectionism that so many of us women wear. This allowed me to truly acknowledge and appreciate my intrinsic value, celebrating every aspect of who I am.

Still, the belief that perfection is the standard for worthiness can be an immense burden on women. Society's expectation to conform and strive for flawlessness is unattainable and detrimental to our sense of self-worth. **Embracing imperfection is an integral part of acknowledging and affirming our inherent value.** Imperfections, whether they are physical, emotional, or related to achievements, do not diminish your worthiness. In fact, they allow for the cultivation of authenticity and genuine experience of life.

Worthiness is our birthright, not something that needs to be earned or validated externally. When you understand that imperfection and worthiness can coexist harmoniously, it dismantles the notion that perfection is a requirement. This liberates women from self-imposed pressures, enabling them to embrace their inherent value and deserving nature.

Also, unfortunately, it's a widely observed phenomenon that women tend to downplay their achievements and positive qualities. Doing so unintentionally hinders their own success by internalizing a sense of unworthiness. Downplaying achievements stems from societal conditioning, ingrained modesty, and a fear of appearing boastful or overconfident – traits that are deemed unattractive in women. By acknowledging and challenging this tendency, however, you can start to dismantle this barrier and break free of the constraints it imposes.

Recognizing the negative impact that downplaying accomplishments can have upon you is the first step in breaking free from it. It requires a conscious effort to challenge and reframe your beliefs. Celebrating your successes and appreciating your talents and unique qualities does not equate to arrogance as you might think. It serves as a catalyst for empowerment.

As I write this chapter, I realize that these words and this chapter are meant for me. Though I have a pretty good sense of self-worth, I do tend to downplay my accomplishments. Even when I publish a new book or receive recognition in business, I seldom share this information with my social group. I might make a post or two on social media initially, but then

I withdraw. I guess I still carry a bit of fear of appearing boastful. It's a delicate balance to strike and something I still need to work on.

It's also important to remember to be kind to yourself, challenge any self-doubt you may have, and allow yourself to acknowledge that you are deserving of everything you desire or have achieved. **When you know your true worth and feel worthy, you don't need anyone else to confirm it.** Your self-worth is determined by you alone. To begin feeling the worthiness you deserve is to remember the wisdom of Wayne Dyer, "Self-worth comes from one thing – thinking that you are worthy." Embrace this notion and feel worthy of everything you've accomplished.

Each person possesses a unique set of skills, perspectives, and experiences that contribute to his or her personal journey. Embracing and celebrating successes and positive attributes is an essential step toward unlocking your true self and achieving success. When you cultivate a strong sense of self-worth, it creates a transformative power of feeling worthy, which reinforces a positive self-image, boosts confidence, and fosters a growth mindset. Nurture your feelings of worthiness, for you truly deserve it!

24

WHAT SUCCESS
Tastes Like

Happiness is the Highest Level of Success.

"Success is like honey; it tastes sweet,
but it can be very sticky. "
Mark Twain

Success is a concept that permeates every aspect of life. It can be described as the achievement of a desired outcome or the fulfillment of your goals and aspirations. While success is often associated with external achievements such as wealth, fame, or recognition, its true essence lies in the personal experience and satisfaction derived from those accomplishments.

First and foremost, **success tastes like satisfaction.** It's knowing that all your hard work, dedication, and perseverance have paid off. It's that moment of triumph when you can finally savor the fruits of your labor. Success leaves a lingering flavor of contentment, as it signifies that you have achieved what you set out to.

Success also tastes like empowerment. It's the feeling of being in control of your destiny, having the ability to shape your future. It ignites a sense of confidence, instilling the belief that you can conquer new frontiers and tackle even greater challenges. The taste of success empowers you to dream

215

bigger, strive harder, and reach even greater heights. It fuels ambition and propels you forward on the path of continued growth and achievement.

Furthermore, **success tastes like gratitude.** It's the humble recognition that success is not achieved in isolation but is often the result of collective support and collaboration. The taste of success is imbued with an appreciation for the mentors, friends, and loved ones who provided guidance, encouragement, and belief in your abilities. It is a flavor that evokes humility and reminds us of the importance of acknowledging and expressing gratitude toward those who have played a part in our success.

Success also carries a taste of resilience. It is a bittersweet reminder of the obstacles faced and the failures endured along the journey. Success often arises from setbacks and challenges, and it is the ability to rise above those difficulties that makes the taste of success more satisfying. It is the taste of strength and resilience, symbolizing the ability to bounce back from adversity and grow stronger in the face of obstacles.

As well success can encompass a wide range of outcomes, both tangible and intangible, that we experience because of our efforts such as:

- The achievement of our goals.

- Financial well-being.

- Desire recognition and reputation.

- Increased opportunities.

- Improved Quality of Life.

- Personal growth and development.

- Enhanced relationships.

- And personal satisfaction and fulfillment.

For me, success is a combination of all the above. It's the satisfaction that I've lived up to my potential and pursued my sense of purpose in life. While success has not always met my lips, it has made its taste more gratifying when it has.

However, within the vast tapestry of human existence, the definition of success is uniquely defined by the dreams, passions, and aspirations of each person. There is no one-size-fits-all mold, as success is as diverse as the individuals that seek it. It can only be defined on your own terms and what gives you true fulfillment.

Success is also not a fixed destination, but a dynamic and perpetual journey. Rather than fixating on a distant endpoint, you can embrace the present moment and cherish the progress made along the way. This becomes the truest marker of achievement and success. By focusing on living purposefully, success becomes an inherent part of your daily experiences and progress, rather than an end goal to be reached.

Ultimately, success is a unique and personal taste that varies from individual to individual. It is not merely a destination but a journey, but by embracing this personalized voyage, you will discover the treasure of self-fulfillment and the authentic taste of success.

25

CREATE A HEALTHY
Lifestyle

You Have More Than You Realize if You Have Your Health.

"It is health that is the real wealth and not pieces of gold and silver."

Mahatma Gandhi

In today's fast-paced and demanding world, prioritizing good health and overall well-being is essential. Various aspects of your health such as self-care, balance, stress management, anxiety, sleep, exercise, and eating habits are all interconnected and form the foundation of your health. While it's unrealistic to expect perfection in these areas, the more we recognize the importance of these factors, the more motivated we become to *want* to adopt healthier practices. All of this starts with acknowledging the significance of self-care. Self-care is not selfish. It's an essential practice of nurturing your physical, mental, and emotional well-being. It helps us create an enhanced quality of life and sets the stage for a healthier and happier you.

Engaging in any activity that promotes your health should become a priority and habit. Areas such as the following are good places to start.

- Eat a healthy diet.
- Get enough sleep.

- Exercise regularly.
- Manage stress.
- Find balance in your life.
- Practice self-care.

Maintaining a healthy diet is essential for optimal physical and mental well-being. By nourishing our bodies with wholesome choices, we experience increased energy levels, a strengthened immune system, and reduced risks of chronic diseases. Additionally, a healthy diet promotes mental clarity, supports mood stability, and contributes to a positive relationship with food. However, I acknowledge the occasional craving for sweets or desserts is also part of being human. I admit, as much as I try to eat healthfully, I love my sweets. When I give in to this temptation, I make a conscious effort to correct my habits the following day. I recognize that no one can be perfect all the time, so give yourself some grace, but aim for most of your days to be filled with nutritious choices and prioritize your well-being.

For many of us women, a balanced diet is also necessary to support a healthy weight. As we age, our metabolism slows down making weight management more difficult. Portion control, incorporating whole foods, and being mindful of added sugars become a necessity. Adopting a healthy diet is a journey that requires patience and commitment. Start by making small, sustainable changes to your eating habits and gradually build upon them. Each step, no matter how small, is a step in the right direction toward achieving healthy food habits.

Sleep is also essential for good health and has a restorative power that is often undervalued in our society. Adequate sleep helps keep your body in peak performance and your mind finely tuned. Most adults need between seven and eight hours of sleep per night. I realize that as we age, this can be more difficult to achieve. Yet, a consistent sleep routine, creating a sleep-friendly environment, and practicing relaxation in the evening can contribute to a restful night. Because I'm an earlier riser, I try and go to bed early most evenings, and I utilize a Bedjet that blows cool air into my sheets, keeping my body temperature exactly where I like it. Some people like a sound machine, a fan blowing on them, or a darkened or cool room. No matter your preferences, make your bedroom as comfortable as possible.

Something else that may help is to limit your exposure to electronics before bed. It's been shown that the blue light emitted by electronic devices such as phones, tablets, and computers can interfere with sleep. Turn them off at least an hour before bed or use blue light filters that can be found in the form of inexpensive glasses on Amazon. Also, avoid stimulants such as caffeine close to bedtime, and try to avoid stressful situations or conversations. By prioritizing sleep, it will allow you to wake up rejuvenated and ready to face the day.

One of my passions is tennis, so finding time on the court three or four days a week is my avenue for exercise. Exercise, regardless of the form, offers a multitude of benefits for both the body and mind. When you exercise, your body releases endorphins, which elevate your mood and reduces stress, it can improve cardiovascular health, build muscle, increase strength and endurance, improve flexibility and coordination, and help you to maintain a healthy weight. Everyone has individual preferences when it comes to exercise, and whether it's a brisk walk, yoga, strength training, or any other activity, the key is to find a routine that fits into your lifestyle. Remember, exercise is about taking care of *yourself*. It's a valuable investment that can have far-reaching benefits.

Moreover, the positive impact of exercise extends beyond the physical and mental realms, permeating into various aspects of our lives. Regular physical activity can enhance cognitive function, boost creativity, and improve sleep quality, contributing to heightened productivity and sharper focus throughout the day. Engaging in exercise often cultivates a sense of disciple and commitment that can spill over into other endeavors, fostering a proactive and resilient attitude in tackling challenges. Additionally, the social interactions that may come with group activities like team sports or fitness classes can lead to new friendships and a sense of community, further enriching the overall experience of well-being.

Stress is a normal reaction to life's challenges. However, when stress becomes overwhelming or prolonged, it can have detrimental effects on your physical and mental well-being. Managing stress effectively is essential for maintaining a healthy and balanced life. Navigating life is challenging enough, but when stress and anxiety are introduced, it can greatly impact our lives. Developing effective stress management techniques can help navigate these times. Mindfulness practices, deep breathing exercises, yoga, meditation, and spending time in nature are all ways to help reduce stress. When you engage in any activity that brings you joy and relaxation, it can reduce stress levels and anxiety. While everyone's stress management techniques differ, explore what works for you and incorporate them into your life when difficult days arise.

The effects of chronic stress extend beyond our immediate well-being, potentially influencing our long-term health outcomes. Elevated stress levels have been associated with a range of health issues, including cardiovascular problems, weakened immune function, digestive disorders, and even an increased risk of chronic conditions such as diabetes and hypertension. Recognizing the interconnectedness of our physical and mental health underscores the urgency of effective stress management. By dedicating time and effort to stress-reduction strategies, you are fortifying your body's resilience against the potential long-term consequences of ongoing stress.

Achieving balance in your life is the ability to maintain a healthy equilibrium between various aspects of your life, such as work, relationships, children, and personal care. When we are out of balance, it can lead to increased stress, anxiety, and feelings of being overwhelmed. To cultivate balance, prioritize activities that align with your values and passions, and set boundaries when necessary. It's okay to say no to commitments that don't align with your priorities or that may overextend you. Remember, it's not about achieving perfection or dividing your time equally among all areas of life. It's about finding what works for you and focusing on the things that truly matter.

Overindulgence in any one area of your life can lead to disharmony while neglecting certain aspects can leave you feeling incomplete. A balanced life allows you to allocate time and energy to your passions and responsibilities without sacrificing your well-being. By setting boundaries, prioritizing self-care, and nurturing meaningful connections, you create a life that flows more harmoniously.

By prioritizing health and self-care, we can establish a solid foundation for our overall well-being. But why have I chosen to include this information in this book? It's because health and self-care form fundamental pillars for overall well-being. Without a healthy body and mind, it becomes more challenging to accomplish your goals and rise to your aspirations.

When we prioritize our health and engage in self-care practices, we lay the foundation for success, enabling us to pursue our goals, overcome challenges, and highlight the significance of investing in ourselves.

Furthermore, focusing on health and self-care serves as a reminder that success and fulfillment are not solely measured by external achievements. True success encompasses taking care of our bodies, nourishing our minds, and fostering emotional balance. Our overall well-being forms the cornerstone of our capacity to excel and make a meaningful impact on the world. Just as an artist requires well-maintained paints and canvas to create their masterpiece, we require a healthy body and mind to live up to our ambitions and achieve our goals. Recognizing that our bodies and minds are the vessels that we navigate our lives, it underscores the importance that this is where the pursuit of success must begin.

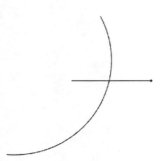

26

BECOME THE BEST SHE-EO OF YOUR

Embrace Your Personal Power and Live the Life You Dream Of.

"The only person you are destined to become is the person you decide to be."

Ralph Waldo Emerson

Every day I find myself pondering a fundamental question: Who do I aspire to be today? While I may be a Gemini who is known for its dual nature, I am not a person with multiple personalities. However, this daily inquiry serves to realign my thoughts and direct my attention toward becoming the person I need to be to pursue my dreams. My goal is to be the best version of myself, and to do this, it takes a mindful awareness of my current state at any given moment throughout the day.

So, who do you have to become at this moment to achieve your goals? It's easy to succumb to procrastination or regress into unproductive habits of the past. Posing this question to yourself can help to reorient your focus and help get you back on track. Often, we underestimate the significance of our actions – the timing, manner, and execution. Yet every action sets off a chain reaction. Therefore, it's important to reflect on whether your actions align with your desires. By consciously shaping your actions, you can chart a path that propels you toward the desired outcome you seek.

Becoming the best "She-EO" of your life means taking charge and assuming the role of a powerful and successful leader, both personally and professionally. Just like a CEO guides a company toward growth and success, you can steer your own life toward fulfillment, happiness, and achievement.

To become the best She-EO you can be, you need to start by defining your vision and setting clear goals. What do you want to achieve in different areas of your life? Whether it's in your career, relationships, health, or personal development, outline your aspirations and create a roadmap to reach them. Just like a CEO develops a strategic plan for their company, you must **establish a plan for your own life**.

Next, **prioritize self-awareness**. Understand your strengths, weaknesses, values, and passions. This knowledge will help you make informed decisions, leverage your strengths, and work on areas that require improvement. Like a CEO who understands the company's internal dynamics, you must have a deep understanding of yourself to make the best choices for your personal growth and success.

Another crucial aspect of being a She-EO is **taking ownership of your actions and choices**. Just as a CEO is accountable for the company's performance, you must hold yourself accountable for your decisions and their outcomes. Take responsibility for your successes and failures, learn from them, and adapt your strategies accordingly. Embracing accountability will empower you to take control of your life and drive it in the direction you desire.

Moreover, a She-EO **understands the importance of continuous learning and development.** Like a CEO who stays updated with industry trends and invests in professional growth, you must dedicate time and effort to expand your knowledge, skills, and perspectives. Seek opportunities for personal and professional development, whether through reading, attending workshops, or seeking mentorship. Embracing a growth mindset will fuel your progress and keep you ahead in your journey toward becoming the best version of yourself.

Additionally, a successful She-EO **knows the value of self-care and balance.** Just as a CEO ensures the well-being of their employees and maintains work-life harmony, you must prioritize self-care and establish a healthy lifestyle balance. Nurturing your physical, mental, and emotional well-being will not only enhance your productivity and effectiveness but also contribute to your overall happiness and fulfillment.

Lastly, a She-EO **supports and uplifts others.** Like a CEO who fosters a positive work culture, you should empower and inspire those around you. Share your knowledge, lend a helping hand, and celebrate the successes of others. By creating a supportive network and fostering a culture of collaboration, you not only enhance your growth but also contribute to the growth and success of others.

In conclusion, becoming the best She-EO of your life is about embracing your personal power, taking charge of your destiny, and leading yourself toward success and fulfillment. You will become what you believe you can become! Become a powerful manifester of your life. **Take action to create the life you want, become an amazing She-EO, and achieve the success and fulfillment you desire.**

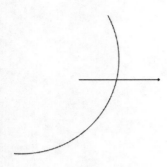

Afterword

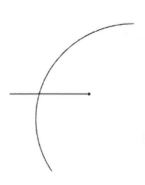

A Bit of Knowledge Can Put You on the Right Path.

As I near the conclusion of this book, several realizations dawn upon me. First, I realize that I stand at the precipice of yet another transformative change in my life – one that demands more changes and personal growth. While my passion for the solar and renewable energy business has burned brightly for the past fifteen years, it no longer satisfies that profound inner longing within me. I wholeheartedly believe in the benefits my business has brought to our clients, and I continue to reap the advantages of solar power in my own home. However, an indescribable force tugs at my heartstrings, and my inner voice compels me to heed its call.

I find myself coming full circle in my life's purpose. During my twenties and thirties, I knew my calling was to assist women by imparting financial knowledge, enabling them to attain greater control over their lives. Regardless of the topics employed to assist them, however, the central focus was always on helping women. Once again, thirty years later, I stand at the junction where a similar desire to support, uplift, and empower women emerges within me. I believe that this book marks the beginning of my renewed journey to fulfilling that purpose.

Though the destination of this path remains uncertain, I embrace the willingness to begin. The prospect of leaving behind the familiar and venturing into the unknown is undeniably unnerving. Yet, it is also imbued with a sense of excitement and invigoration. The opportunity to pursue uncharted territories fills me with a thrilling anticipation that propels me forward.

I express sincere gratitude for the investment of your valuable time in exploring the ideas and narratives presented within these pages. Your dedication is truly valued and deeply appreciated, and I wish you a life's journey filled with only success and fulfillment.

Please feel free to reach out to me at any time and share your path. I would love to hear from you.

Ivy

Email: ivy@ivygilbert.com
Website: ivygilbert.com

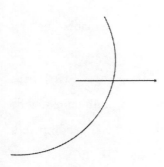

About the

Author

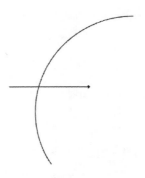

Ivy Gilbert is an entrepreneur with four decades of invaluable business expertise. Throughout her career, she has founded and grown several multi-million-dollar companies and start-ups. Her knowledge spans finance, management, sales, and business development, complemented by experience in mergers and acquisitions, franchising, and taking companies public. She has been a CFO, a CEO, and a full-time SHE-EO.

For the past fifteen years, Ivy has immersed herself in the hyper-growth industry of solar and renewable energies. She propelled this venture to become one of Florida's most respected solar energy companies, earning recognition as one of *INC Magazine's* fastest-growing private companies in America and being named one of *Solar Power Magazine's* Top 500 Solar Contractors in the United States for ten years in a row.

While involved with all these companies, she also nurtured her creative side by writing several books of her own and dozens more for others. "It gives me great pleasure to see how people appreciate my writing, but frankly, I would still write even if no one read my books because it's the process that I truly love."

Finally, she cherishes quality time spent with family, and playing tennis with friends.

"I can be a very busy woman," Ivy states, "but as the saying goes, '*If you want something done, give it to a busy person. The more things you do... the more you can do.*' That seems to be me in a nutshell."

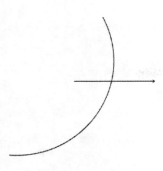

How can I
Help You

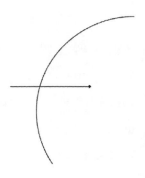

How can I help you in your journey toward becoming a She-EO and achieving a life of success and fulfillment?

Regardless of whether you are an established business owner experiencing growing pains, just starting out on a new business endeavor, or wanting some help in your personal She-EO endeavors, I can help you on your journey. Sometimes all it takes is a little inspiration, an accountability partner, or a fresh set of eyes to review the situation. There is also great power in a sharing community. I have multiple ways you can interact with me and get all the help you need. I would consider it an honor to assist you on your journey.

NEWSLETTER

Sign up for my free newsletter for lessons and tips to help you to reach your full potential as a She-EO and learn how others are achieving success through our community.

PRIVATE COACHING AND CONSULTING

No matter where you are on your journey, I have probably been there as well. I offer a free 20-minute call to discuss ways in which we might work together. My coaching fees are very reasonable, and scholarships are available if money is an issue. My goal is to help you achieve exponential growth in all aspects of your She-EO life.

AUTHOR ASSIST

Author Assist is my copyrighted program to help you get the book you have inside of you published and out and into the world. As someone who has written several books of my own and dozens more for others, I have broad experience in what it takes to complete and turn a manuscript into a book. If you have a valuable message you want to get to others, I can help you avoid the mistakes that most new writers make. In the end, you will have achieved your dream of being a published author.

SHE-EO MASTERMIND COURSES

These are extensive programs I offer online to anyone who is ready to challenge themselves, pursue a life of purpose, and achieve their dreams. I offer these exclusive courses in affordable, self-paced learning programs. They are the easiest way to begin a journey of self-discovery and awareness to help propel you to new heights of success and fulfillment.

SHE-EO RETREATS AND WORKSHOPS

Our three-day "Inner She-EO" retreats are being designed to help you reset and focus. Our time together will be engaging and fun with presenters that will help you break out and experience true She-EO greatness. More information will be announced in our newsletter as these programs progress.

ADDITIONAL COPIES OF *UNLEASH YOUR INNER SHE-EO* FOR YOUR BUSINESS OR ORGANIZATION

If you are interested in multiple copies of my book to give as gifts to your employees, team, or friends, please contact me. Discounts are available based on the number of books ordered.

HELP ME HELP OTHERS

If you obtained something of value from reading *Unleash Your Inner She-EO*, I would appreciate your telling others about it. You can also share your thoughts by writing a review on Amazon. Reviews are tremendously helpful in a book's success and impact on the world. To review the book simply log into your Amazon account, locate the book, scroll down to the Customer Review Section, rate the book, and then write a review. Thank you in advance, and I sincerely appreciate you!

LET'S START THE CONVERSATION

Send me an email or reach out on Linkedin or Facebook to ask questions or discuss ways we might be able to work together. I look forward to helping you.

> Email: ivy@ivygilbert.com
>
> Website: ivygilbert.com
>
> Facebook: https://facebook.com/IvyGilbertMedia
>
> LinkedIn: https://www.linkedin.com/in/ivy-gilbert-798a879/

Notes

Introduction

Page 4 *Women CEOs of the S&P 500*: (2023, February 3). Catalyst.

Page 4 *FORTUNE Announces 2023 FORTUNE 500 List:* (2023, June 5). FORTUNE Media.

Page 4 *Women in the Fortune 500: 64 CEOs in half a century:* (2023). Carpenter, Julia. CNN Money.

Page 4 *Historical list of women CEOs of the Fortune Lists: (2023, June 22). Catalyst.*

Page 4 *Women in Business Statistics, Facts, & Trends:* (2023, July 9). Yaqub M. (CBC). Data & Research.

Chapter 6

Page 55 *The Neuroscience of Presentations*: (2019, Oct 4). Manta. Bogdan. Neuroscience for Business Expert.

Page 57 *Time Use:* (2020). Esteban Ortiz-Ospina, Charlie Giattino and Max Roser. OECD Time Use Database. https://ourworldindata.org/time-use.

Page 57 *American Time Use Survey:* (2023, June 22). US Bureau of Labor and Statistics.

Page 57 *Media usage in the U.S. - statistics & facts*: (2023, June 19). Guttmann, A. Statista.

Chapter 7

Page 64 *The Harvard MBA Business School Study on Goal Setting*: Wanderlust Worker.

Page 67 *SMART Goals: Specific, Measurable, Attainable, Realistic, Timely:* CFI Team. CFI.

Chapter 8

Page 73 *You're The Average Of The Five People You Spend The Most Time With*: (2012, July 24). Rohm, Jim. Business Insider.

Page 73 *The Success Principles*: (2005) Canfield, Jack with Janet Switzer. Book.

Page 73 *Healing the Hardware of the Soul*: (1989.) Parade.

Chapter 13

Page 117 *How Many Times Does the Average Person Move*: (2020, April 30). Grant, Isaac. https://www.verifiedmovers.com.

Page 118 *How Many Jobs Does the Average Person Have*: (2023, January 11). Kolmar, Chris. Zippia. https://www.zippia/advice/Average-Number-of-Jobs-in-Lifetime/.

Page 118 U.S. Bureau of Labor Statistics: (2022, September 7). https://www.bls.gov.

Chapter 14

Page 130 *Parable of the drowning man:* Wikipedia. https://www.en.wikipedia.org/wiki/Parable_of_the_drowing_man.

Chapter 21

Page 181 *Think and Grow Rich:* Wikipedia. https://en.wikipedia.org/wiki/Think_and_Grow_Rich.

Page 184 *Tesla, Inc*: (2023, August 9). Brittanica. https://www.britannica.com/topic/Tesla-Motors.

Page 184 *History of Tesla: Timeline and Facts:* (2020, October 5). Reed, Eric. The Street. https://www.thestreet.com/technology/history-of-tesla-15088992.

Page 184 *Tesla's Entry into the U.S. Auto Industry:* (2019, May 1). Sull, Donald. MIT Management Sloan School. https://mitsloan.mit.edu/teaching-resources-library/teslas-entry-u-s-auto-industry.

Made in the USA
Columbia, SC
24 July 2024

38616547R00146